JOURNEY INTO UNDERSTANDING

ANNE ARNOTT
as a young girl

JOURNEY INTO UNDERSTANDING

by
ANNE ARNOTT

With a foreword by
THE ARCHBISHOP OF YORK

MOWBRAYS
LONDON & OXFORD

© Anne Arnott, 1971

Printed by offset in Great Britain by
Alden & Mowbray Ltd
at the Alden Press, Oxford

SBN 264 64567 7

First published in 1971

CONTENTS

ILLUSTRATIONS

FOREWORD BY THE ARCHBISHOP OF YORK

FROM one point of view, *Journey into Understanding* is a period piece. It takes us back to the early decades of the twentieth century, with glances further back into the nineteenth. This alone gives the book a value, for in a fast moving world we can all too easily lose the picture of how life was lived at the end of the Victorian age and in the years of Edward VII and George V.

But the book is far more than a period piece. It is a spiritual autobiography told with reticence and with a deep sensitiveness. As the writer developed into womanhood, she left behind the religious restrictions and conservatism by which she had earlier been surrounded, and found her feet set in a larger room. She might have been somewhat embittered by the experiences through which she and other members of her family had passed. From this she was saved by the deep love and respect which she had for her father, even though she came to differ deeply from him in her approach to life in general and to religion in particular.

In this book there is an entire lack of that bitterness which characterises Edmund Gosse's *Father and Son*, though there are similarities in the tales that are told by the two writers. Here we see the development of a spiritual life in which not a little suffering has issued in a depth of understanding and a richer faith.

I am grateful for the book, for its humour and its restraint.

It will, I believe, have a word for some who fear to launch out into a braver religious world, and a word for those who might lapse into bitterness because of the restrictions under which they themselves were brought up.

Bishopsthorpe, York   DONALD EBOR

PREFACE

To my father's family I must have seemed an intruder, my arrival late and untimely. Yet they never said anything. If only we had been able to talk, it might have been easier. But we conversed on the surface, and played out our days around the central figure who dominated us all.

My father was a doctor, a consultant physician, and I was the youngest of his three daughters, the only child of his second wife. Born during the First World War in a Georgian house in Bath, where a stream of patients came daily to his consulting-rooms, I was a small child in a world of adults.

It was an unusual home, ordered and sober in its routine, and because of my father's character, remote from the social life around us. He was a man with a passion for God, and he walked through life as if it were a pilgrimage. Puritan in nature, undeviating and relentless in his faith, his years were spent in pouring out the concentrated power of his remarkable healing skill on all who needed it. When things went well, you could see a radiance in his eyes, and he walked with a light and buoyant step. He was often an enigma to the world around, and sometimes to his family. He was a Plymouth Brother.

When I recently described, in another book, a small part of all that happened, I never thought that the publication of those brief memories of a childhood among the Plymouth Brethren would bring so many moving letters from people in all parts of the world who now felt free to reveal certain memories, to share not dissimilar experiences, and to express doubts and questionings which still haunted them. So often the underlying theme of all they wrote was the same: the mysterious problem of the closeness between good and evil, so that sometimes the one inexplicably seemed to give rise to the other, and those who were irrevocably linked by ties of love often hurt each other the most. Why is this so? Often it was in homes where the Christian faith was fervently held, that people were alienated from each other. In so far as the warm secure fellowship of family or church became an exclusive group, it turned away many who needed its accept-ance and support, but who could not, conscientiously, accept all its beliefs and practices. Today Christianity is still often rejected by those who hear the proclamation of the love of God, but who see everywhere barriers between people who should most surely be united, for they profess to follow the same faith.

Strangely, an old leather album of faded photographs of my father's family, spanning a hundred years, began a journey towards understanding. For here in miniature, these problems leaped to life, as I looked at the faces of the people gazing up at me, and recalled what I knew of all that hap-pened. Yet I remembered how, transcending all, shining goodness was seen. Like the strong beams from a lighthouse revealing stormy seas, it stretched out and illumined the lives of some in the picture.

I believed some part of the answer lay in the character of those who were inescapably involved in those far-off events. As a detective gathers clues, so I collected fragments of information, threads of memory, to enter a world forgotten, and see it through the eyes of those who had peopled it. Many lie on the hillside now, dust to dust and ashes to ashes. Their sorrows and joys are forgotten. Their quick voices are silent. But as I studied them again, I knew they had something to say, and I was the last who could tell their story.

Ryton-on-Tyne,   ANNE ARNOTT
March 1971

ACKNOWLEDGEMENTS

MATERIAL for this book came from varied sources. The books listed in the bibliography, and also family papers and letters, helped to uncover the fascinating period between 1860 and 1920. I am, moreover, deeply indebted to those of my father's patients who wrote and described him to me as they had known him; to Doctor Gordon Spear of Bath, who, at his own suggestion, took the trouble to collect memories of him from various people; to Mrs Martha Baker who assisted him, and whose memories of the family are still so vivid; and to my sisters for recounting certain recollections of their childhood. But the main part of the book is the record of one person alone.

During its writing I owed much to the encouragement and advice of certain friends, notably Mrs Jean Coggan and Mrs Eileen Cornwell; and to Mrs Rachel Lucas for her swift and expert typing. But I could never have completed it without the good humour and patience of my own family as I wrestled with the manuscript, and the unfailing help of Canon William Purcell.

The book is dedicated to all those who asked for it.

A. A.

THOMAS

I

THOMAS

Who is this stranger, unknown and yet known? He seems so alive that I feel as if he might suddenly step right out of the picture and into the room. It is, I realise, a striking face. The thick dark hair and heavy beard and side whiskers give an impression of patriarchal strength. The brow is broad and lofty as it might be that of a philosopher. He is clearly a Victorian. The well-cut grey cloth jacket whose revers are edged with braid, and the large bow tie, might have been worn by any professional or business man in the middle of the nineteenth century when this small daguerreotype must have been taken.

It is the eyes that hold me. They look steadily into the distance, penetrating and a little sad. I saw them a long time ago, gazing at us from a large picture in my father's bedroom. They seemed to watch with compassion the man who lay there at the end of his life, whose thoughts had turned with a strange devotion to the moment when he would see his father again.

So I am standing on the threshold of the past, ready to begin a search for understanding. I am looking at Thomas, my grandfather, of whom I have heard much. I wish I had known him, for I have often wondered what made him so strangely compelling a man that every one of his eight children wanted to please him, and regarded him with a love and a devotion that seems unusual even in those days of the

1

stable Victorian family, when the father was often a figure to be unquestioningly venerated. Yet it cannot, I think, always have been easy to live with him.

Thomas was in one sense a radical, a passionate seeker after truth, a protester against those things he held to be wrong. His restless conscience led him to take his stand among the despised and unpopular, but, as he said, he was willing, even privileged, to be 'a fool for Christ's sake'. He was a man of the Book, called less amiably by some 'a Bible-puncher'. Such men are apt to be rugged and independent, and in this he was no exception. Like Martin Luther he could say, 'My conscience is captive to the Word of God'. Yet, because of this, he was eventually to build around himself and his family an invisible citadel, from which some of them never came out again. It was a spiritual edifice, build for conscience sake. In this lay both its strength and its weakness.

He belonged to a London family, most of whom lived in or near Blackheath. They were the successful owners of a 'confectioner's' business, which manufactured patent medicines, 'curiously strong peppermints' and tiny black menthol lozenges, which up to this day are still made, and packed in similar little bright-coloured tins, which can be carried conveniently in a handbag just as they were in Victorian gentlemen's waistcoat pockets. Thomas, only of his family, had no desire for the busy world of commerce in south-east London, and he chose to become a gentleman farmer as it was then called, because of his passionate love of the countryside and of the whole world of Nature whose marvels were, to him, so clear evidence of the miraculous power of a loving Creator. Independent in this choice, he was never content to take opinions second hand. But he shared with his brothers a lively concern at the great problems of the day, and an awareness of the stirring times of change in which they lived.

His family were devout and regular churchgoers, belonging

to their parish church. But in this setting he asked endless questions, and challenged conventional attitudes and beliefs. He had a burning desire for reality and sincerity in all he did. This affected his religious belief. Where was the zeal of the early apostles who had turned the world upside down, he demanded. As he grew up, he had heard many discussions about disquieting conditions in many churches, where there was much injustice in the distribution of clerical wealth, and there were many parishes where the parson was hardly ever present. He remembered his mother telling him how feelings ran so high in 1831 when he was a tiny child that angry mobs had stoned the carriages of certain bishops, and at Bristol, not far from the home of some of his relatives, the episcopal palace had been set on fire, because it seemed that some of the wealthy prelates were not concerned to put things right. He grew up to discuss around the dinner table the seriousness of the unrest among many zealous churchmen, which, in part, gave rise to both the evangelical revival and the Tractarian movement. It was during the former, while attending a great evangelistic meeting, that his own faith took on the intensity and depth that was never to leave him. He was concerned too about the great social evils of the day, so brilliantly mirrored in the novels of the new writer, Charles Dickens, whose books he read avidly as they appeared. Injustice and inequality he could not tolerate. Eventually he was to become a convinced Liberal in politics.

As a young man he farmed for a time in Lincolnshire, and here he met the large family of a squire-landowner. At first they seemed an almost overwhelming family. There were fourteen young people, lively, positive and vigorous, and their home, Swineshead Abbey, was full of laughter, movement, argument, and endless coming and going. The parents were a God-fearing couple, and like him, regular attenders at the parish church. They had sent their older boys to be educated at Rugby under the great Dr Arnold whose ideals and beliefs they so admired. He was a kind of legend in the family, and was often discussed among them all. The squire was fond of telling how Dr Arnold was fearless in his denunciation of slackness in the Church and how in 1832, regardless of episcopal disfavour, for he was himself an Anglican priest, he had thundered, 'The Church of England as it now stands, no human power can save'.

Two of the squire's brothers were vicars, one of the great parish church of St Botolph, known as The Stump, in Boston, then a busy sea-port, and another of the village church at Gosberton just beside the hall which had been the family home until the grandfather of the fourteen children had lost his money by some rash speculation in Welsh mines. These two vicars had been much concerned with the laxity and carelessness of the Church throughout East Anglia, and the whole subject had become a burning issue of the day among the members, young and old, of this large family. They were fond of describing the manifest injustices in the organisation of the Church, which were heightened in East Anglia where the Bishop of Ely had an income of £30,000 a year for himself, and his sons and son-in-law received £4,000 a year each, while half of the curates in England received less than £60 a year each, and lived in poverty. As the years went on, a few prophetic voices had been heard, from men courageous enough to say what they thought, and to set a pattern of true piety and devotion. One of these, Edward Stanley of Alderley, a most dedicated priest, was appointed Bishop of Norwich in 1837 where he remained for twelve years until his death, and the tremendous efforts he made to reform the Church in East Anglia were an inspiration to the outspoken squire's family, who heard much of him through their uncles, and various relatives in Norfolk.

Thomas as a young man, visiting constantly at Swineshead

Abbey, shared in the ferment of thought and the questioning fervour expressed there by a number of the young people. It was here that he read Dr Arnold's book, *Principles of Church Reform*, which was discussed from time to time, in which Arnold put forward his idea that all sincere Christians could be united in one Church. This view was very attractive to him. As an evangelical he believed that it was the soul of man that mattered, and that the power of Christ to transform and convert a man depended not on any one Church, but simply on belief in the forgiveness of sins through the atoning death on Calvary. He did not therefore agree with the Tractarians, High Churchmen who held a more mystical view of the Church, and whose growing influence lay in the persons of such great men as John Keble, Professor of Poetry at Oxford, Edward Pusey, Professor of Hebrew, Bishop Wilberforce of Oxford, son of the great evangelical reformer and emancipator of the slaves, and the brilliant John Henry Newman who had left the Evangelicals, became Vicar of St Mary's in Oxford, and ultimately, surrounded by the clamour of a great controversy, left the Church of England in 1845 to 'go over to Rome'.

It was just after 1850 that Thomas turned his thoughts more and more consistently towards one of the younger daughters of the Lincolnshire family. Jennet was the eleventh child and eighth daughter, and has been described as kind and gentle, but having a certain lively humour which appealed to the young farmer. She may well have been bewildered by his passionate hopes and fears for the Church. But she sensed his sincerity. She could share with him his love of the countryside, and as they walked and talked together under the great oak trees around her home, she enjoyed his sudden laughter that lightened the seriousness, his ridiculous love of practical jokes, his fund of riddles, and above all the vitality and enthusiasm which made him concentrate as fiercely and attentively on every little creature, every bird, beast and insect, as he did on his faith. Life was to be lived to the full, and he was deeply interested in his world. Sometimes he read to her from the monthly instalments of Mr Dickens' new novel, *David Copperfield*. She listened as he discussed the social problems of the day highlighted so fearlessly by Dickens in his books.

At this time there was a great public figure in England whom Thomas much admired, although not always agreeing with his politics. He often discussed with Jennet the indefatigable work of Anthony Ashley Cooper, Lord Ashley, who in 1851 became the seventh Earl of Shaftesbury. His untiring care for the poor and oppressed appealed deeply to him, for he too was very concerned for the evils and injustices seen throughout society. Shaftesbury's factory reform measures, his Mines Act which had earlier prohibited the iniquitous employment of women and children under thirteen in the pits, his leadership in the Ragged Schools, among multifarious other activities, were the more fascinating to Thomas, as he explained to Jennet, because he also shared his evangelical beliefs, behind which lay a true humanitarianism. There was, moreover, a fascinating rumour about Shaftesbury, which my grandfather had heard, and about which he wished to know more. It was said that, from time to time, he quietly slipped away from his great London home on Sunday mornings to attend a gathering of Christians of various denominations who met in a private room together in what was described as apostolic simplicity 'to break bread and remember the Lord'. There was a growing number of such groups spreading across England and on the Continent. They had sprung up like wildfire in the 1830s and 1840s, largely, at first through the remarkable and dynamic leadership of John Nelson Darby, godson of Admiral Nelson, and a priest in the Episcopal Church of Ireland. The members of this movement were called the Plymouth Brethren, for although the first such gathering had been in Dublin in 1825, Plymouth was one of their chief places of origin in England.

John Nelson Darby, the most colourful and influential of the early leaders of the Brethren, was a strange intense character. One of the most vivid descriptions of him was later written by Francis William Newman, brother of the famous John Henry, who was eventually to become the Cardinal. F. W. Newman was the Professor of Political Economy at Oxford, but in earlier days he had stayed in the same house in Ireland as Darby, who immediately had a powerful effect on him, as he describes:

'A most remarkable man—. . . rapidly gained an immense sway over me. I shall call him "the Irish clergyman". His "bodily presence" was indeed "weak"! A fallen cheek, a bloodshot eye . . . a seldom shaven beard, a shabby suit of clothes and a generally neglected person, drew at first pity, with wonder to see such a figure in a drawing-room . . . .

'He before long took Holy Orders, and became an indefatigable curate in the mountains of Wicklow. Every evening he sallied forth to teach in the cabins, and roving far and wide over mountain and amid bogs, was seldom home before midnight. . . . Such a phenomenon greatly excited the poor Romanists, who looked on him as a genuine "Saint" of the ancient breed. . . . That a dozen such men would have done more to convert all Ireland to Protestantism than the whole apparatus of the Church Establishment was ere long my conviction. . . . He had practically given up all reading except that of the Bible. . . .'

During the years that followed, Darby left the Established Church because of his 'pain at the divisions among Christians', and his dislike of worldly ambitions within the church. This is ironical in view of the fact that over the years he himself was to cause the most barren and bitter controversies and divisions among his followers by his extreme autocratic leadership and his rulings over principles of gathering. But the movement started with a new and exciting freshness for thousands of people who were searching for Biblical methods of worship, and the straightforward proclamation of the gospel of redemption from sin.

At first Jennet was uneasy at the way Thomas's thoughts were moving. She was happy in the Anglican Church for she was not given to restless questioning as he was. For her home had been happy, and its piety, fostered through the parents, was never oppressive. Her brothers were allowed great freedom and initiative. Religion seemed a natural background to life rather than a cause for heart-searching. Nevertheless, Thomas fascinated her as none other, and when at last he proposed to her, she did not hesitate, feeling then, as she was to do all her life that he was so clever that all his judgments must be wise and right. She knew, too, that in all he did, he looked for God's guidance first.

She was twenty-three when they married and set up their home together, and Thomas committed their lives and plans to God. Did my grandmother ever quail as a young woman, I wonder, as she watched Thomas continue his restless search for a Church where he could find a fellowship as full of fervour and conviction as were the early Christians in the gatherings described in the Acts of the Apostles?

Soon the young couple moved farther south to farm nearer London, and two small girls were born. Here the pattern of life changed for them.

It was somewhere near Hemel Hempstead that Thomas found the little meeting of men and women who had come together from various denominations. There were several High Churchmen as well as dissenters, yet they were determined to break down barriers and meet together as fellow

Christians who had experienced conversion through faith in
Christ. Their simple worship gripped him, its freshness and
sincerity were exactly what he had long been seeking. Here
were people who met for no other reason but that they 'loved
the Lord'. His heart, in a not dissimilar way from John
Wesley's in Aldersgate Street many years before, grew
'strangely warm'.

Thomas had found his spiritual home for life. Here, he
decided, he would bring up his children, here he would
worship in simplicity and truth. Jennet, who throughout her
life showed great loyalty to all her husband's decisions,
accepted that he had apparently been 'led of the Lord' to
take this step. It was thus that my grandparents, single-
hearted and fearless of the opinion of the society of their day,
joined the Plymouth Brethren. Puritan and uncompromising
this group undoubtedly was, but the members were motivated
by genuine love for each other. There was an unbreakable
bond between them. Looked at askance by the world, they
sat Sunday by Sunday on the hard seats in 'The Room', and
passed from one to another the bread and the wine in
memory of the Lord. They had no liturgy, and read only the
Bible. Apart from the singing of a few devotional hymns,
there was a reverent stillness in the meeting each week, and
all together, and in expectancy, they waited upon God.

Prosperity did not come to Thomas, and he went through
times of anxiety in his farming at this period. Eventually
with the greatest regret he returned with his young family to
London, to take up his rightful position as a partner in the
family business. Sad at heart at leaving the country he loved,
he established a home in quite a handsome terrace house in
Blackheath. Here the five little girls, who had been born in
quick succession, looked down from their nursery window
towards the pond on the heath where children sailed their
model yachts. They were watched over by Etta, their young

nurse, and they quarrelled and laughed and fought as any normal family will.

It was not until the autumn of 1864 that the parents at last had their prayers answered. They had always longed for a son, and it had seemed that their desire would be unfulfilled. But one blustery October day when the autumn leaves were swirling over the heath the children—restless because the maid and Etta were busy and occupied carrying cans and kettles of boiling water up the stairs, and seemed to have forgotten them—saw a carriage draw up outside the front door below. A tall gentleman in top hat and frock coat, carrying a dark leather bag, came up the path at a run, and disappeared inside the house. It seemed a long time later that their father came quietly into the nursery, took the youngest child, Margaret, onto his lap and sitting by the fire drew his little flock around him.

'Let us give thanks to the Lord', he said without preamble.

'You have a little brother. Shall we ask God to bless him all the days of his life?'.

As five heads bent, dark hair mingled with fair and auburn in the firelight, and Papa, kind and godlike, seemed, as the children were often to say in later life, the nicest father in the world.

2

WILSON

THE character of Wilson, who had been born on that October day in 1864, the only boy in a large family of six, later seven sisters, was moulded by two great influences: the character and beliefs of his father, who was puritan in nature, warm and enthusiastic in relationships, and an idealist who could never compromise; second, by the great city in which he grew up, a place of violent contrasts and acute and pressing social problems, where the foremost thinkers of the day were engaged in a crisis of belief no less serious for them than that of today for twentieth-century man.

Blackheath, where he was born, was a pleasant suburb not far from Greenwich Park where the deer roamed through the glades and across the rolling grassy slopes. His home was near the heath itself which was a place of excitement, for there you could ride on the donkeys if you were lucky enough to have a penny, or you could watch the gypsies in their encampments if you were out with a grown-up. You could feed the ducks on the ponds, or race and chase across the grass with a bat and ball. To the end of his life he was to remember his home, and tiny incidents flashed across his mind like scenes portrayed by a magic lantern in vivid colours, so that he could describe them as if they had happened only the day before; and always in his heart he was a Londoner, and in memory he could walk again the streets he had known so well.

11

London in 1864 was a city of shocking inequalities between rich and poor. There was the wealth and opulence of the West End where the 'carriage folk' drove out on summer afternoons; and the splendid horses and highly polished vehicles, dazzling in the sunshine, swept by full of fashionable ladies in brilliant silk dresses holding up ornate parasols, and whiskered men in white top hats and formal dress suits.

A certain John Hollingshead, an essayist, wrote passionately in leading journals of the other side of the picture. In 1864 his writings were fuel for those with a social conscience. He describes the back streets and hidden courts in the same West End, which 'make us doubt our humanity and civilisation'. At the back of the main thoroughfares were tall dingy blocks of dwellings approached only by narrow passages and alleys 'like the mouths of ovens, whose roots lie soaking in stagnant cesspools'. Here pallid starving ragged children crouched and played on top of rotting vegetables. It was a place where epidemics decimated the numbers of those who lived in the sordid tenements. Leech, the cartoonist, drew one of his most powerful pictures in the same year entitled 'A Court for King Cholera'. The crowded slums behind Great Russell Street known as 'The Rookery' are minutely drawn in their dismal squalor. Here cholera raged, for the Public Health Act of 1848 empowering action by local municipalities was not fully implemented until the 1870s. Cheap or common lodging-houses were often a fertile seed-bed for the spread of the disease, and only after Lord Shaftesbury had established certain model lodging-houses, which proved immune to cholera, was action taken to order regular inspection of the trouble spots.

Tuberculosis or 'the white plague' was rampant. Diphtheria and typhoid fever appeared at regular intervals, often causing large numbers of people to be affected.

Manufacturing his patent lozenges and medicines, Thomas, my grandfather, was a student of current medical knowledge, and put many preventive measures into practice to keep his family healthy. Water which could carry typhoid was boiled; hygiene and cleanliness were scrupulously observed. The children were encouraged, somewhat against their will, to take cold baths to 'fortify the system'. As he grew older, Wilson heard his father discussing the marvellous medical advances of the day: it was actually in 1864 that Louis Pasteur established that wine went sour because of a tiny micro-organism transmitted through the air, and thus the germ theory of disease, which is the foundation of modern medicine, was discovered; the new antiseptic methods of Lister, who had studied the discoveries of Pasteur, were found to be effective, and were published in the *Lancet* in 1867; surgery progressed slowly but surely; and Elizabeth Garret Anderson became in 1865 the first woman medical practitioner in Britain after showing a fierce determination to become qualified in face of almost insuperable difficulties. Her achievement was a triumph. Change was in the air, and the medical world was shaken to its foundations. The Crimean War, which has been called 'a foolish expedition', brought terrible suffering to the wounded men, but it also brought one good consequence. Florence Nightingale's astonishing work led to the institution of nursing as a profession for intelligent and often dedicated women.

Thomas, in this changing world, was fascinated by other developments of his day, and drew his children into his interests. Rural England, which he had loved, was shrinking because of the rapid growth of the railroads. It was 'The Railway Age'. He was torn between dislike of the increasing urbanisation of the countryside, and an almost childish delight at the marvels of steam. He drew beautiful sketches in minute detail of many great engines for his children,

Wilson in particular. He had had to leave the countryside, but he utilised the railways to return to it with his family. Both the coast and country were, in fact, now opened up in an entirely new way to the middle-class family man. There was another reason why he deliberately took the children away at regular intervals both for the day and for regular family holidays. It was to have 'a change of air'. Like many thinking Victorians he regarded the Industrial Revolution in part as a sad development, for belching chimneys had polluted the atmosphere, and in South-east London the smoke from end-less rows of depressing cheaply-built houses for the workers often filled the sky with a pall that hid the sun. It was, therefore, wise to fill the lungs from time to time with the sweet invigorating air of moorland or shore. He organised regular expeditions to coast and country. There were over five thousand miles of railroad in England by the time Wilson was born, and the choice of places to go to was varied. It had become customary to travel by rail for any long distance, although a great variety of horse traffic supplemented the railways.

The sea-shore had become a place of exciting discovery, and Thomas sometimes took his flock for a holiday by the cheap express train to Ramsgate, and thence by carriage to Broadstairs. With a magnifying glass in his waistcoat pocket he would stroll across the beach, ready to pick up and examine the smallest sea creatures, starfish, sea anemones, sea-urchins or shells. The seven small girls, dressed in their check gingham dresses, and the little boy in his sailor suit, clustered around their father, pushing, wriggling, peering at the latest marvel; or else they raced and ran across the shingle, or climbed onto the old wooden pier, which was often battered in the winter gales. The girls vied with each other in collecting strands of different types of seaweed, skilfully floating very thick paper under the specimens to lift them

out of the water, and drying them out later. Then they
placed them in home-made books of thick white paper. One
of these has been preserved to this day, and the colours of
the feathery seaweed are only a little dimmed as each piece
lies carefully arranged, fixed to the page with strips of
gummed paper. In the neat copperplate writing of a child, a
verse is inscribed. The whole flavour of the book is remote
from the world of today, full of undertones from the past, for
the child who fashioned it grew old and died long ago. The
written words are worth recording:

'Call us not weeds, we are flowers of the sea
 For lovely and bright and gay tinted are we,
 And quite independent of sunshine or showers
 Then call us not weeds, we are ocean's gay flowers.
 Not nursed like the plants of a summer parterre;
 When gales are but sighs of an evening air,
 Our exquisite fragile and delicate forms
 Are the prey of the ocean when washed by the storms.'

The railways, which made sea-side holidays possible, were
promoted in the public eye almost as a moral benefit, one
which it behoved every family to patronise. *The Official
Illustrated Guide to the South Eastern Railway and its Branches* by
Measom, published in 1858, had urged the desirability of
train journeys in words which seem strangely alien in temper
to us today, but which show how opinion was being moulded
to a new age:

'The wide extent of varied sea-coast, offers opportunities
to the vast numbers who inhabit London which cannot be
overrated, both as regards moral and sanitary influences;
and the interior of Kent—aptly called the Garden of
England—as well as Surrey are rich in rural allurements.'

Such pious and idealistic phraseology was common at this

time, for religion permeated many areas of thought, and even
the frieze over a certain London bank had the words inscribed on it 'Lord direct our labours'.

The fervent often evangelical faith so prevalent among the
middle classes went hand-in-hand with awe and respect in
face of the treasures of land and sea. For many Victorians,
and Thomas was here typical, were passionate students of
natural history, tracing in the wonders of creation and the
development of life all the signs of an omnipotent Creator.
With faithful eyes they perceived miracles in every natural
event; in the butterfly emerging from its dark chrysalis; in
the birth of a lamb; in the unfolding of a flower. One well-
known author, describing London, wrote, 'how much there is
to be seen and done, even by a working-man, within a day's
walk of smoky Babylon itself; and how easily a man might,
if he would, wash his soul clean for a while from all the
turmoil and intrigue, the vanity and vexation of spirit of
that "too-populous wilderness", and by going out to be
alone a while with God in heaven, and with that earth which
he has given to the children of men'.

The author of those words was a certain Canon Charles
Kingsley. Strangely enough, it was in a children's book that
he was able to show distaste for the worse effects of the great
growth of industry. It was published in 1863. The little girls
were delightedly reading it in the Blackheath nursery at the
time their brother was born. It was thought to be a suitable
book for them because it highlighted the harsh differences
between the great open world of nature and the dirt of man-
made factories and mean houses. It revealed the very wonders
they enjoyed on the sea-shore. The book was *The Water
Babies*, and the tone was moral and improving with a deeply
religious note. Kingsley described his aims in a letter to a
friend, and his words are typical of the beliefs held by many
Victorians, whose faith was fortified by the contemplation of

God's works. 'I have tried in all sorts of queer ways', he writes, 'to make children and grown folks understand that there is a quite miraculous divine element underlying all physical nature. . . . And if I have wrapped up my parable in seeming Tom-fooleries, it is because so only could I get the pill swallowed by a generation who are not believing with anything like their heart, in the Living God.' Kingsley felt that, with the wonders of machines and of new inventions, there was a danger that man was losing God. He is at pains to trace in the book the painful contrast—for him—between the natural and the man-made world.

Wilson was born, then, in an age of change, and in a city of glaring social evils. London was as bad as anywhere. Kingsley's story of the little Yorkshire chimney-sweep who learned to be clean was relevant in more ways than one to South-east London. Little children were still employed as 'climbing-boys', and Blackheath and Greenwich were bad areas where they were still steadily used. Thomas rigidly opposed such cruelties and brought up his family to do the same, and read aloud Hollingshead's *Essays and Miscellanies*, both to Jennet as she sewed and mended under the gaslight, and to the older girls. 'Dozens of such children die of consumption', he read. 'They get up to their work in all weathers, and often at two or three in the morning. Most masters prefer to take their climbing-boys very young, as they learn more readily. Six years is considered a nice trainable age. At first they will come back with their arms and knees streaming with blood, and the knees looking as if the caps had been pulled off. Then they must be rubbed with brine . . . and go off to another chimney.' The words were quoted from those of a master sweep who repented of the system. It was not until 1875 that the law became really effective in stopping the evil practice, and then it was through the influence of Lord Shaftesbury, whom Thomas so admired. Thomas's care and concern for the welfare of children was unusual at a time when only one child out of two was having any formal education, and for many the slum streets were the only place for them to play.

Outwardly this was the age when religion was the respectable concomitant of middle-class affluence and stability. Poverty was often ignored. Nevertheless, the picture held today of the Victorian age as being one of unquestioning belief in Providence, and of evangelical piety in the middle classes is one-sided, for the climate of thought into which Wilson was born was as turbulent in some respects as it is in this generation. Stormy winds of doubt and discontent were blowing through traditional strongholds, and eventually there were not many who would be totally unmoved by them. The gale was rising in different quarters.

In the year of Wilson's birth a young man, expelled from France for his dangerous political beliefs and activities, was spending his days working in the British Museum, studying and writing. His profound knowledge of economics became such a weapon in his hand that it cut like a rapier through accepted thought patterns, and such strife was caused by it between the privileged and the non-privileged, that the clamour of battle was heard throughout the world, and still continues. The man was Karl Marx; his book was *Das Kapital*, which appeared three years later. Thomas was a liberal in outlook and had something of the reformer in him, and he was concerned for inequalities of wealth. He lived extremely modestly compared with other owners of commercial enterprises and factories. Luxuries were never encouraged. He was much aware of the poverty of those who lived down near the river and in the East End. A tenth of his income was regularly laid aside to alleviate need or to help missionary enterprise. In later years he was to become an ardent advocate of Free Trade under Gladstone, which lifted the weight of taxation from the poor. Sick at heart at 'man's inhumanity to man', he often turned his thoughts to the simplicity of the country life he had left behind. A great reader, he was in complete agreement with much that was written by Matthew Arnold, son of the great Doctor, and at the time of his son's birth Professor of Poetry at Oxford. He did not agree with his advanced somewhat radical religious beliefs, for so they were considered, but he did feel at one with his lament for the passing of rural England as he understood and knew it, and like him he felt city life was unhealthy.

Arnold in *The Scholar Gypsy* alluded to it as,

> 'this strange disease of modern life,
> With its sick hurry, its divided aims.'

Life had indeed, it seemed, become a mad rush. Great developments in trade and industry fostered through the railways on land and the use of steam instead of sail, and iron instead of wood in the mercantile marine at sea, built up great pressures in the expansion of trade. The efficiency of business was increased by new and wonderful developments such as the Electric Telegraph which already had a number of offices in London, and by the speed of written communications which now could go by the penny post.

These dramatic changes went alongside a formidable upheaval in religious thought. The very foundations of secure accepted belief had been shaken by the publication, five years before Wilson's birth, of Darwin's *Origin of Species*. The faith of churchmen and believers in the inerrancy of Scripture was subjected to the severest and most alarming test. The Genesis account of Creation had always been accepted as literally true. It was 'The Word of God'. Now, dreadfully, it occurred to unlearned people in the Christian Church that the precious 'truths' they had been taught were false. It does not seem to have occurred to them that their literal interpretation might have sometimes been mistaken, and that they were not studying a book of science, but a book which marvellously revealed a spiritual picture of man's early struggles. The man in the pew, who was not a student, felt that his faith was undermined, and the great and needless controversy of Science versus Religion began, the echo of whose clamour has still not died away. It was from the year of Wilson's birth that the great controversy raged. For in 1864 *The Times*, the chief organ of respectable opinion, published a leading article on the matter, and the public seized on the idea that geology contradicted Genesis, and the Bible was untrue. The question of evolution became of burning importance. In the same year Disraeli made a bold statement to the Oxford Diocesan Society with all the power of the true orator that he was:

'The question is this—Is man an ape or an angel? My lord, I am on the side of the angels.'

His statement was greeted with prolonged and thunderous applause.

A profound shock had been also caused by another book, *Essays and Reviews* published in 1860 and written by seven Oxford scholars, six of whom were clergymen. It seemed to attack the very foundations of belief. Although the quality of the essays was uneven, that by Jowett, Master of Balliol, was particularly disturbing in that it combined love of the Bible with apparent disbelief in its inspiration. His exhortation 'to read Scripture like any other book' brought consternation among the clergy. If it did nothing else, the noise of battle surrounding the conflict of views, united Tractarians, Evangelicals and old-fashioned liberals as never before, but the damage had been done. In the year Wilson was born, the Roman Catholic Cardinal Manning, who had formerly been the Anglican Archdeacon of Chichester and a close

associate of Newman, thundered in Rome in front of a
number of cardinals:

'The Church of England sits in her chair mute and con-
founded.'

It was left to some of the great Cambridge scholars of the
day, theologians and historians, to try and preserve calm and
stability, and to draw order out of chaos. Westcott and Light-
foot, both to become in their turn Bishops of Durham, and
Hort who was both a scientist and a theologian, fearlessly
attempted to present new insights in a scholarly manner,
while not ignoring the conclusions of scientists and archaeolo-
gists. They did much to bridge the supposed chasm between
science and religion. But their apparently calm appraisal of
the crisis of belief was not given without a personal struggle.
They had had to face another fact. For many the decision of
Newman and Manning to leave the Anglican church in the
1840s had been a serious blow. When, in 1864, Canon
Charles Kingsley actually attacked the personal veracity of
Newman and the attitude to truth of Roman Catholics in
general, in an article in *Macmillan's Magazine*, another older
controversy was fanned into flame after it had smouldered for
nearly twenty years. It was in 1864 that Newman's powerful
yet poignant *Apologia Pro Vita Sua* was written, in answer to
the attack. It traced his life in the Anglican church through
the stages which led him to the Church of Rome. Its obvious
sincerity and truthfulness did much to clear Newman of the
charges levelled against him, but left the difficulties of
reconciliation between those who held differing doctrinal
beliefs no easier. It was to some a distressing book. Westcott
went through a time of perplexity; he wrote to a friend in the
same year:

'My summer was not as fruitful as I had wished; or rather
it was not fruitful in the way I had wished. Dr Newman's

Apologia "cut across it", and opened thoughts which I thought had been sealed for ever. These haunted me like spectres and left me little rest.'

Eighteen hundred and sixty-four, the year Wilson was born, could almost be called a watershed. It was a time when, perhaps as never before, men wrestled with doubts and perplexities. Perhaps because of this, or perhaps as a sign of defiance in face of the marauding hordes of those who seemed to be attacking most precious beliefs, there was, alongside the confusion, an upsurge of evangelical fervour. There was a great increase in the number of those who, like Thomas some years earlier, shook the dust of the Establishment off their feet and departed into the ranks of dissent. They held firmly, some said blindly, to their own concepts of the inspiration of the Bible, convinced that there must be some flaw in the reasonings of man and in scientific theories; they argued convincingly that there was undoubtedly 'a missing link' in Darwin's theory.

Thomas, whose final departure from the Anglican Church had been caused by the 'unitarian outlook' of his vicar, who seemed to belie the divinity of Christ, felt happy and at peace at this time with the Brethren whose whole lives bore witness to the *certainty* of their belief. If questioned as to the reason for this, they had an irrefutable answer: 'I *know* Whom I have believed . . .' and in every event of their lives they claimed to trace the divine and guiding hand, and answers to prayer so remarkable that there was left no room for doubt.

By now the Brethren movement was established in Switzerland, France, Germany, Canada and the United States of America, largely through the indefatigable ministry and endless journeys of John Nelson Darby. Already, however, great conflicts had risen among his followers in England. Certain individuals and 'assemblies', as they were called, were in disfavour with him for interpretations of doctrine. He assumed the most autocratic control, and an almost papal authority. As a result, many autonomous assemblies with more liberal attitudes left him, and eventually these became known as the 'Open Brethren'. Ultimately, the followers of Darby were to be called 'The Exclusives'. In spite of this, the movement grew in numbers and vitality, carried on as closely as possible to the New Testament practices of the early Church as they were understood from Scripture. The Brethren had one advantage. Their freedom from any rigid ecclesiastical structure, any set liturgy, and their supposed freedom from the pre-eminence of any one man—although this was often an imaginary freedom—left them ready and waiting to listen for the guidance of the Holy Spirit, and to worship in simplicity in a setting and atmosphere that, at its best, could only be described as totally uncluttered. Stripped for action in mind, they met in rooms and meeting halls which were bare indeed. There is no doubt that there was an outpouring of spiritual emotion that was deeply sincere. They had bypassed the formal structures of ecclesiasticism, and claimed they had found reality and truth.

A number of notable names appeared in their ranks, generally of men who rejected higher critical scholarship because they maintained the Scriptures were the '*living*' Word, which could never be analysed by men as in a labora-tory, for eventually and always it would prove its own truth. One such was Thomas John Barnardo, converted in a Ply-mouth Brethren meeting hall in Dublin. In 1864 he was a member of the Sidney Street meeting in Stepney; and it was from the ranks of the Brethren that he took many of his first helpers in his epic rescue work among the 'lost' children of London's underworld. Ultimately he left the Brethren to work in a more liberal setting.

Another great evangelical movement, whose influence

WILSON

was to be profound, was emerging at the same time, in the person and thought of one man in 1864. In that year William Booth began his great work which was later to culminate in the founding of the Salvation Army.

It is clear, then, that Wilson was born at the moment of time when there was a great movement by leading evangelicals as well as high churchmen towards both social concern and spiritual reality. Here, in his own way, Thomas, his father, took his stand, and interested himself in the Ragged Schools, and in the conditions of London's poor. As he held his tiny fragile son each evening in his arms, he commended him in prayer to his Lord, to spare him if that was the Divine Will, and to strengthen him, so that he might bring healing and comfort to those in need. Above all he asked that the Lord would 'work mightily' through him so that in whatever he did, souls would be saved.

This was the great city, this the home and the climate of thought, in which a small delicate boy grew up. He was lively, alert and impatient, quick in perception, stimulated by every interest, and Victorian London was full of fascinating sights and sounds. He had a gift of intense concentration, and with it all he was dogged, obstinate, and affectionate. His sympathies were easily aroused, for he was as warm-hearted as his parents.

Here in a little faded photograph he sits on the edge of a chair, three years old perhaps. He is pale and a little perplexed, probably because he was forced to keep perfectly still and was urged not to move a muscle while he watched the photographer vanish behind the large box camera on its tripod. The man's head had surprisingly vanished beneath the enveloping black cloth. He was told to watch for the dickey-bird, but hard as he looked, no bird ever appeared. So he is fixed there in the photo, watching and waiting. His white socks hang wrinkled on thin legs, and he is dressed in 'petticoats', like other little Victorian boys, which for him meant a checked gingham dress with a double line of braid around the hem.

It was obviously a tiresome way of spending the afternoon. He had waited while his five elder sisters were photographed, and now there was only Edith, the baby, to have her portrait taken. She was to be seated on the lap of her grandmother who was dressed in her best dress, a smart black watered silk, trimmed with braid, and who was wearing her white lace Sunday cap. Although Edith was an exceptionally determined child, she was cheerful and placid unless opposed in some wish, and now she sat beaming happily around, a plump little girl perhaps not quite two years old. So here is Wilson, pictured on that day, and a moment of the past is recaptured for posterity. Lucy, the prettiest of them all, was not yet born. (In the other photos Annie looks anxious and responsible for she was the eldest, and had to help Mama keep all the younger ones quiet. Jennet smiles a little wistfully and Mary looks sad, remote, disinterested. Alice has a secretive look behind a rather forced little smile, and Margaret looks sweet-tempered, eager, and lively.)

The childrens' home was certainly a place of plain living and high thinking. Bread might be spread with butter or jam, never both. Meat, contrary to the general custom of the day, although taken regularly, was eaten in moderation. The water in the brown hip baths, placed regularly in front of the coal fires in the bedrooms, was often cold, and the children were plunged briskly in and out, and rubbed in coarse towels until their skin glowed. They were taken to no entertainments, no theatres, no dances. School work had never to deviate from the very best, for no slacking was allowed. And over and above all else there were the religious routines. Family prayers, a very widespread custom in middle and upper class homes, were said each day, the father expounding a passage of Scripture. Grace before meals was never missed. On Sundays the family sat together on the hard wooden chairs or benches in the meeting, morning and evening, listening to the 'ministry' of one brother and another. Some were tedious, and often they grew exceedingly restless. If their father spoke, he held their attention immediately.

Such was the diet of this lively family. If it seems a remarkably heavy one to less disciplined modern minds, then one is left asking why the eight quarrelsome high-spirited children never rebelled against their parents. The memories of them all, expressed years later, tallied on this point. Was it because theirs was a happy united home, enlivened by the many great gatherings of large families of cousins of a similar age—there were over sixty on their mother's side alone —and stimulated by the talk, the arguments, the discussions, the games in which they all shared? Or was it because they felt keenly and instinctively the caring love of their parents?

The outstanding events in the childhood of Thomas's son, which in later years were still vivid in his memory, were unusual, and may seem to some distinctly surprising.

The first concerned a traumatic experience within himself. It was, remarkably and unmistakably, his own conversion at the age of six years. The actual spark that ignited the flame of a living faith, which burned steadily and unceasingly through Wilson's life, was struck in the nursery at Blackheath by the young nurse, Etta, who in the manner of the nineteenth-century evangelicals, cared for the souls as well as for the bodies of her young charges. A tiny woman, strong-willed and dominating as Wilson later described her, she ruled the nursery with discipline, love, and the telling of Biblical stories in no watered-down version. In after years Wilson never forgot the moment, incredible perhaps to some materialistic minds today, when he gave 'his heart to the Lord' in his sixth year at the knee of his nurse. He had asked her what the Crucifixion was. She, arm around him, told of cruel and wicked men who had nailed to the Cross the Saviour of the world, who had died there for him, for He had taken on Himself the sins of all men, so that they might be reconciled and redeemed to a righteous God. Her story must have been vivid, even violent in the telling. The small sensitive boy saw, felt and wept at the terrible scene.

'My tears ran down', he said unaffectedly in later years, 'and I cried to Etta, "Why did they do it to him?" "For your sins and mine", she answered, so I asked her what I must do.'

And the nurse told him how he could ask forgiveness for all he had done wrong, and could then give himself, his life and talents to the One who so greatly loved him. The small boy, then and there, knelt down and asked the Lord to take him and make him His.

'I have never regretted that day which I truly believe saw my conversion', he used to say in recalling that memorable moment.

He even remembered the black American cloth cover of the Bible given him by his parents at that time, and the fact that when he subsequently read aloud to Etta the gospel narrative of the Crucifixion, she wept. It was in this manner that he took the first decisive step of his life. From that moment he set out on a journey from which he never turned back. He had become one of those who seek a heavenly city and a vision of inexpressible beauty, and he followed resolutely behind his father.

From that time onwards he walked with the great biblical thoughts of forgiveness, salvation and redemption echoing through his mind like a joyous peal of bells.

His second memory was of fear. While on holiday at Broadstairs after an illness, he was taken for a drive along the sea-front in a carriage. He sat beside his Mama and

Annie. Presently the sky grew dark. Mothers and nurses gathered their children off the beach and hastened towards the houses. The slow plodding horses dragged the bathing boxes away from the edge of the sea into the shelter of the sea wall or the pier. A violent thunderstorm broke overhead, while mother and children were sitting in the open carriage. There was no place of shelter. They had no umbrella. The rain was torrential, the forked lightning terrifying, and there was some way to go to their lodging. Water poured off the shining cape of the coachman on the box in front of them, and the children, soaked and terrified, clung to their mother.

'I remember I was much alarmed', Wilson said, recalling the day many years later, 'but Mama committed us to the Lord, and mercifully we were not struck by the violent lightning, but I was thankful to get safely home.'

The picture of the stoical mother, sitting upright and composed in the carriage, calmly offering up a prayer for protection in the storm, while the nervous horses quickened their paces, was indelibly printed on his mind for life.

It is, certainly, a strong present-day fallacy to regard the Victorian home as essentially forbidding and dull, and its moral atmosphere as stifling. In fact, the good home, even if extremely authoritarian, was often lively, full of initiative and originality, for with none of the diversions of today's mass media the large families concocted many enterprises and entertainments among themselves.

Wilson was allowed to keep many pets. He inherited his father's love of natural history, and so there was the faithful dog, the lame bird, the white mice, and the little bright-eyed guinea-pig who, he wrote years later, was allowed to sleep in the warm kitchen on winter nights by the glowing embers of the fire in the coal-black range. Cages for the little animals were home-made, and often experiments were attempted. On one occasion, helped by his father, Wilson fashioned a tiny peep-hole in the wooden side of the mouse-cage, so that the daily development, growth and progress of the babies arriving so regularly in enormous numbers could be noted, recorded and studied from the time of their birth. His father, who could entertain as well as instruct, caused the children immense delight by his mischievous practice of curling their pet grass snakes around his wrists hidden under his cuffs when visitors arrived. As he shook hands, he contrived to allow the snakes to slither down to the appalled shock of the person whom he was welcoming.

On winter nights Thomas instructed his children to put on woollen mufflers and assemble around him in the garden, or follow him out onto the heath. Here Wilson especially was instructed to look through the telescope at the marvels of the universe, as his father pointed out now Orion, now the Pleiades, and now the Plough, or the constellations in the dark velvet of the night sky above nineteenth-century London. The brilliance of the starlit heavens never left the mind of a boy who, like his father, had begun to perceive the unfathomable wonders of God's creation.

Whenever the wind raced and roared across the heath, and the autumn leaves swirled in clouds through Greenwich Park, kite-making began. Fashioned from very stout brown paper and home-made wooden cross-bars, the kite was carried outside, and the children, holding the ball of thick string attached to a piece of wood, let it eddy up crazily, hither and thither into the turbulent air, higher and higher, until it soared away above the tallest trees, tugging at their hands as they ran shouting and chasing its erratic wild flight.

Reading was encouraged. Books were often restricted and moral in tone, or confined to natural history. Certain books of the former type were objectionably full of forced piety. Deathbed scenes, and almost sadistic disasters recounted in order to provide warnings and admonitions, were not in-

frequent. But the children had some of the great classics, and
were avid readers of Dickens. Thackeray's *The Rose and the
Ring*, *Robinson Crusoe*, and *Gulliver's Travels* were favourites,
as was *The Swiss Family Robinson*. Lighter fiction was considered frivolous and undesirable. To this was added the
objection that it bore no stamp of *truth*. This was a particular
offence to a number of the strict Brethren who became so
rigidly exclusive in their reading that they became entirely
out of touch with the world around them.

On the other hand, all creative and practical work was
encouraged. Wilson remembered vividly all his life the very
hard cold winter when a whole room had been turned over
to him so that he might work indoors at advanced carpentry,
and a clever cabinet-maker came to teach him. Here he had
drawn to scale the sketch plan, elevation and section of a
summer-house, which he painstakingly made in sections,
and with pride he saw its completion and erection in the
garden, where it stayed for years, and it was taken down and
re-erected at every subsequent move.

He had been born into a family of restless lively children,
who reacted on each other like unpolished gems, sometimes
rubbing uneasily together, too sharp for comfort. Yet they
were deeply attached. The sorrows of one were the griefs of
all, and so it was to be throughout life, and the mellowing
years would polish and soften the jagged edges.

What cemented the unbreakable relationships in this
family? What kept them almost blindly loyal to their father's
beliefs? True, two of the sisters joined the Church of England
in later life, but it was, in one case anyway, only a superficial
severance of loyalties. Does the answer lie, I wonder, in the
character of the father? He was the potter, they the clay in his
hands, and he fashioned the vessels to his own pattern with
the loving care and precision of a craftsman. When he had
gone, they were fixed in an unbreakable mould. His stamp

was upon them. Outwardly they appeared unlike each other in looks and nature. But there was that inner acquiescence to him. Their minds had been bent to the will of one man, and they were content that this should be so. Thus the storms of doubt and disbelief around them passed them by. Their father's assurance became theirs.

Is it, I sometimes ask myself, the prerogative of parents to mould the characters of their children? The Victorians, who regarded the breaking of a rebellious will as an integral part of training, nevertheless produced many characters of remarkable strength. The borderline between guidance and domination is narrow. Some of the eight children, who grew up so different, ultimately retired into a small and secluded world of the spirit. Nor did any of them stray from within the well-defined boundaries mapped out for them in childhood, and illumined by the faith of their father.

Through their eyes I can picture them yet. It is a Sunday evening. Their gentle mother is sitting at the piano, and as her hands range over the keyboard the melody spills out softly into the room, and she looks up at the group around her and smiles. The tall vivid father, with the black hair and beard, is standing with his arm around the small pale boy, who is eager and taut as a coiled spring, restlessly moving, hopping a little as the music urges him. The shifting cluster of girls are grouped around the piano beside them, their faces determined, lively, their hair a pattern of colours from dark to auburn and light brown. The tune is taken up by their voices as they stand in the gaslight which hisses and splutters gently. For a moment they are irradiated, caught in the glow of light, like a kaleidoscope pattern of colour and movement, and the moment is held in the mind for ever, while they sing together with a strange and touching simplicity:

'I think when I read that sweet story of old,
  How Jesus was here among men,
  How he called little children as lambs to his fold,
  I should like to have been with them then.'

THE MEDICAL STUDENT

3

THE MEDICAL STUDENT

HE looks ahead as steadily and resolutely as he did long years
later when he was the strongest influence in my life. Here is
the man who was to become my father. What was he thinking of, I wonder, as he sat there, young, still and reflective,
while the plate camera caught the rigid pose and captured the
mood of a moment? He wears the well-cut clothes of a late
nineteenth-century professional man, a jacket of good cloth,
a crisp wing collar and a large silk spotted necktie. His heavy
moustache, worn according to the current fashion among
many Victorian men, does not fully conceal the firm set of
the mouth. There is tenacity there, doggedness, obstinacy
even, in the set of the jaw and the tilt of the head. But the
eyes are kind, and there is a steadfast quality in the expression.

Wilson, the small delicate boy, had grown into a pale
energetic young man, aged twenty-four at that time, and he
had just graduated as a Bachelor of Medicine at the University of London in addition to passing the qualifying
examinations which he took at Guy's Hospital. The photograph was necessary for applying for posts, and I surmise he
found the process a tedious waste of time.

In imagination I can picture him as he sprang up from
the chair, free to examine the camera with interest, and chat
to the photographer at the same time, for he was interested
in all inventions, and he was later to develop the more

35

efficient keeping of accurate records of medical case histories by having patients photographed in different stages of certain diseases, particularly those affecting the skin.

I can see him as he ran down the steep staircase from the photographer's room above a shop, and walked out into the winter sunlight filtering down through the mist onto the streets of the Borough. As he walked quickly along with a light springing step as if his thoughts buoyed him up, he noted the signs of poverty all around him. He was both saddened and challenged as he looked at the mean streets, the dark alleyways and the crowded dirty thoroughfare whose cobbled road echoed to the clatter of the hooves of horses as they trotted past, drawing the cabs, the double-decker buses, the tradesmen's drays, and carts coming into London with vegetables and country produce. Sometimes by contrast, the glossy immaculate carriages of the medical specialists swept by swiftly, driven by neat coachmen towards Guy's or St Thomas's Hospitals. Inside the top-hatted men were formally attired in morning suits. They may have looked elegant, but often they were tired men working under great pressure in most depressing conditions, and they were accustomed to see death so frequently that they had to learn to harden themselves or else they would have been overwhelmed.

Threading his way along the crowded muddy footpaths where street vendors were selling their wares, he watched barefooted children race in and out of side-streets, while some sat pale and listless in dark doorways. Many of them were thin and stunted, and their legs were bent with rickets; and some were lame, and his quick mind raced ahead, assessing possible tuberculosis of the hip, or perhaps malnutrition. He studied them as he passed with concentration and care, for children were always to be one of his chief concerns. Even then, his mind worked on the possibilities of improving the milk supply or teaching slum mothers to boil all milk, and these ideas he was to put into practice later. Only seven years before it had been discovered that milk carried the germs of many diseases including typhoid fever, scarlet fever and diphtheria as well as bovine tuberculosis, four deadly diseases of the time which were very prevalent in the poor parts of South-east London. Wherever he walked, his eyes took in every detail around him, and he stored away material for future use.

From time to time his attention was diverted to the street entertainers. The barrel organ player stood in the gutter, his instrument grinding out its rather melancholy melodies, and around him a crowd of little ragged children had gathered. Farther on, three men with blackened faces and American-style hats stood together tapping their toes in time to the notes of the penny whistle, banjo and accordion on which they played minstrel songs. He always enjoyed the simplest entertainment as he walked by, watching everything.

Near the great hospital in St. Thomas' Street, a little bare-foot boy stood selling matches out of a tray hanging suspended with a cord around his neck, and a group of Cockney women with tattered shawls around their shoulders stood beside baskets of fresh flowers. He bought a tiny bunch of violets for a very sick woman in one of the wards. Nearby a young boy poorly dressed, his shrewd little face pinched with the cold, knelt on the path beside the railings of the hospital with an upturned wooden box in front of him, with his shoe blacking brushes on it. The boot-black looked so cold that Wilson stopped and let him polish his shoes and gave him a coin before he went through the imposing iron gates and entered the great entrance court of Guy's Hospital. Swiftly he crossed the flagged paving stones, and passed by the statue of the founder of the hospital. The sculptor had caught so vividly an expression of shocked sadness and concern on the face of the man that some said he had a 'melancholy cast of countenance'. It had been induced, it was thought, by recollections of the terrible misery and suffering he had seen around him in the area in the late seventeenth century which had caused him to found the great institution noble in conception, which bears his name, and which was originally built for the many 'incurables' he saw in nearby St Thomas's Hospital, of which he was a Governor.

Thomas Guy had been a bookseller and publisher, and the manner of his life and his aims were entirely in line with the ideals and beliefs of Wilson, and Thomas his father. Because of their admiration for the founder, they had always had a special regard for this hospital. One of Guy's early ventures in particular pleased them as they had read accounts of it. Owing to the poor quality of Bibles printed in England, Guy had been one of a number of booksellers who encouraged the importation of beautifully produced Bibles from Holland which were, through their efforts, brought over to England in vast numbers. He was a deeply religious man whose great desire was to make the Bible available at a low price to every householder in the land. Although the Dutch venture was stopped after a time, he and Peter Parker, another publisher, eventually were made printers to Oxford University in 1678. During those years they fulfilled Guy's great wish and provided well-printed copies of the Bible at a cost that could be afforded 'by the humblest householder'.

He was a munificent man who helped the poor in many ventures, none greater than the founding of the hospital completed in 1725 for 'four hundred poor persons or upwards, labouring under any distempers or disorders, thought capable of relief by physic or surgery'.

It was a foundation that grew steadily greater and broader in scope through the eighteenth and nineteenth centuries and the spirit of the place had appealed to Wilson when he grew old enough to turn his thoughts to a career. His interest in

medicine had been a natural result of many talks and discussions with his father about the marvellous discoveries that
were taking place as he grew up during the years when he
was an eager hard-working schoolboy in a private school
at Blackheath. During those years Pasteur's findings included
the successful immunisation of sheep and cows against the
deadly disease of anthrax which occasionally infected people.
Lister's triumphs in aseptic and therefore safer surgery were
so great that they were to cause a French doctor to say to
him later: 'You have driven back death itself'. The new
developments in anaesthetics were fascinating, and since
Queen Victoria had accepted chloroform at the birth of her
son Prince Leopold in the eighteen-fifties, great strides were
being made in their use. The Middlesex Hospital had, in
fact, appointed its first anaesthetist in 1874.

Coupled with his intense interest in this progress—an
interest which was shared by his father, who was still engaged
in the production of antiseptic and soothing lozenges and
various wholesome medicaments—was the powerful influence of his home. Wilson had grown up to accept and understand the strict routines and the puritan outlook of his father
and mother simply because, I believe, his parents were
totally sincere, and devoted to their children. He had watched
his father's compassionate concern for the sick and the poor
which caused him steadily to 'lay aside' part of his income
each year for the alleviation of suffering. He saw his father's
zeal, too, to bring the gospel to them.

Wilson was convinced that there was meaning and reality
in his father's Christian practices, and this now coloured his
whole life. He had become a convinced Plymouth Brother,
toughened rather than weakened or made hostile by the
régime at home, puritan in outlook, quiet in speech, but
with an inner strength that stemmed from his own strong
faith, and a boundless energy that enabled him to face

challenges, tiredness, and difficulties with remarkable
resilience. He had become a friendly young man with an
easy approach to strangers and children, and an immediate
interest in everyone to whom he spoke. He had a habit of
getting into conversation with anyone whom he happened
to meet on a train, in the street, in a shop. All through his life
he was to strike up easy relationships with chance acquaintances.

When finally his idealistic desire to serve both God and
man had culminated in his decision to qualify as a doctor, he
entered Guy's Hospital as a student in 1883, and thus he
hoped he might learn how to alleviate some of the suffering
so clearly evident in the slum districts of London. He was not
alone in his family to have this ardent wish. Annie, his eldest
sister, had been fired, too, by the discussions at home with her
father and brother. She and two of her sisters had become
teachers in a girls' private school in Blackheath, but suddenly she gave it all up to go and train as a nurse at St
Bartholomew's hospital in Smithfield. On her hasty visits
home by horse-bus or train, she flew in and out, always in a
hurry, a small bustling animated young woman, full of
stories of life as 'a lady pupil' at the hospital. Women like
herself, who entered what was in effect a new profession for
those of 'gentle birth' as it was then termed, largely through
the untiring efforts of Florence Nightingale, were often chosen
to become the hospital sisters. Nevertheless it was an arduous
daunting life for any but the resolute. The working hours of
nurses were exceedingly long. Food was often poor and
unappetising. The nurses stood as they were taught, in
groups, in the wards to which they were assigned. They were
dressed in long ankle-length dresses, covered by white aprons,
and wore cotton bonnets tied under the chin.

Annie, from a gentle if strict home, now found herself
surrounded by cases of extreme gravity. In the dark nights,

the wards, which were fitfully illuminated by dim and flicker-
ing gaslight, echoed to terrible groans and cries. People only
went to hospital when it was thought they were almost past
help, and it was a last and desperate resort. But Annie was
not deterred. She was not her father's daughter for nothing,
and she shared her brother's enthusiasm for the new advances
in medicine. She wanted to be in the thick of what was being
achieved. But in one way she was going on a different path.
She loved to slip into the ancient church of St Bartholomew
near the hospital, sometimes to pray for a very sick patient,
sometimes to collect her own scattered busy thoughts. She
began to move away from the standpoint of the Plymouth
Brethren. But Wilson, like his father, was essentially independent in outlook, and had not her feeling for tradition. He
had grown to believe that through Bible reading, meditation
and prayer, and the taking of the sacraments at 'the Lord's
Table', he could learn God's message to man without any
intermediary and without set forms of worship. As a student,
one of his relaxations in the little spare time he had in the
late evenings, was to study under the gaslight in his tiny
dresser's room looking over the front square of the hospital. In
addition to his medical work, he was teaching himself the
Greek of the New Testament because it was closer to the
original words of Scripture. As he sat there, sometimes joined
by another student, a certain Walter Fisher who shared his
beliefs, he pored over the text, and let his mind relax into the
great eternal message of the gospels. Here, I believe, he
gained the calm and inner peace to tackle the difficulties and
face the sadness in much of his work.

He was fascinated by surgery. It was no obvious choice, for
in summer the dissecting-rooms had no refrigeration, and
working conditions were most unpleasant. Then students had
to learn to look at tragedy apparently unmoved. During his
first years at Guy's, several outstanding men among the

younger leading physicians died from illness and probably
the effects of overwork. The cases he attended in the wards
were extremely serious. Like his sister, he may have been
shaken in spirit, but not in resolve, and he became more
determined to increase his knowledge at every point.

This conscientiousness brought him unusual recognition
as a student. He was given post after post of special responsibility, each one coveted by many other men. He was made
Surgical Clinical Clerk, Dresser in the Casualty Department,
Medical Clinical Clerk, Assistant Surgeon's Dresser, and
Obstetric Clinical Clerk. He was sent out into the Borough
to attend cases of desperate illness. He became dresser to the
Senior Aural Surgeon, and finally dresser to the great
surgeon, Mr Davies Colley. This meant that he accompanied him everywhere, walking with him through the long
surgical wards, working in the operating rooms with him, and
assisting in all cases of difficulty or emergency. Mr Davies
Colley had been a brilliant Classicist at Cambridge before he
came to medicine, and he encouraged the young student who
was teaching himself Greek in his spare time. He was a
strong character, outstanding in wisdom in dealing with
hospital affairs, and a brilliant surgeon, respected and trusted
by everyone, and loved by his students. He later wrote of
Wilson that he was 'an able and successful student in the
medical school', that he had charge of 'many serious cases of
accident and disease', and was 'very kind and attentive to the
patients'.

Wilson had another opportunity to work with an out-
standing surgeon. This was the young American, Mr.
Charters Symonds, who made history in 1883 by removing
the appendix, between attacks, using Lister's aseptic methods.
Wilson became officially Aural Surgeon's Dresser to Charters
Symonds who was placed in charge of a new Department for
Diseases of the Nose and Throat in 1886 and became an

authority on the subject as well as continuing general surgery. It was at this time that the first operation of excision for carcinoma of the larynx was ever performed, and Charters Symonds carried through this most difficult operation to a successful conclusion. It was Wilson of whom this brilliant man wrote, 'I had no hesitation in leaving the most important cases under his care, having the fullest confidence in his judgment and ability', for he added, 'he was one of our most successful students'.

During the years when he was a student from 1883 to 1888, Wilson used to go home to Blackheath whenever he got a brief time off from his work, and see his family. Sometimes he discussed his future with his parents. Perhaps it was at this time that the father saw in the son the possibility of achievement he had longed for, but had never had the opportunity to fulfil. Did he long to have the spiritual satisfaction, I wonder, of sparing one of his family to go out as a missionary to evangelise in those parts of the world where the gospel of Jesus Christ had never been heard? In his son, he may have seen a vision of both the healing of broken bodies and the saving of souls. I believe he expressed his thoughts to his son in stirring terms, and the young man was fired by his own desire to give up everything, if need be, for Christ's sake. Also, in many ways Wilson longed for adventure. Often when he got a short time away from the hospital, he walked down to Greenwich and watched the towering masts of the great ocean-going clippers against the sky, and sometimes as they headed down river he saw their sails bellying out as they took the wind and headed swiftly towards the open sea. He watched the new steamships carrying greater tonnage than ever before since goods were now carried to the ports by means of the railways. Sometimes he crossed to the other side of the Thames on the ferry boats so that he could watch the crowded water traffic, feel the wind in his face, and smell the distant indefinable tang of the sea carried up to the heart of London. The breeze ruffling the grey water always aroused the restless longing in his mind to travel to foreign lands. He talked it over with Walter Fisher, his friend, who shared his ideals, his faith, and his determination to qualify with the highest honours. The sorrows of London's poor were acute, but he began to feel they were as nothing to the tragedies of Africa or China where there was so often no medicine for the sick, and no healing for the souls of those who had never heard the name of Jesus.

He had often talked with Walter Fisher about Africa. While the two men were students, he used to go to Walter's home in Greenwich from time to time, or else Walter and his sister Harriet visited his home at Blackheath. Africa through these years was in their minds, because many courageous men had gone out from the Brethren meetings as pioneer missionaries to a strip of land from the coast of Angola to the border of what is now Zambia with Mozambique. Many had died there of hardship and disease. The need for doctors was desperate. So many men, in fact, were lost there that the land became known as 'The Beloved Strip'.

It was in 1881 that a young man of twenty-three called Frederick Stanley Arnot, a member of the Plymouth Brethren in Glasgow, sailed for Durban, and set out for the interior from there. He intended to make for the Zambesi, and follow it to one of the watersheds on the north, where he expected to find mountainous and healthy country where a centre for missionary work could be established in far better conditions than before. Often as many as fifty per cent of all missionaries going to Africa had died in the low-lying mission stations along the river banks. The health of Arnot's companion broke down in Durban, and so the young man set out alone and was lost to sight for seven years. In 1888 he at last arrived back in England to find himself a hero, after amazing adventures only paralleled by those of Livingstone, and hair-breadth escapes, so that he had often been at the point of death. *The Times* described him under the heading 'A New African Explorer':

'His outfit was of the most slender character. He travelled practically unarmed. He was almost everywhere received with friendly welcome by chiefs and people, who clearly appreciated his confidence. . . .

Mr. Arnot struck north-west (of the Barotse) through that wonderful country of rivers, to Bihé. The hydrography of this strange region he has helped to unravel . . . One thing he seems clearly to have proved, that Livingstone's Leeba, coming from the north-east, is the real Zambesi . . .'

Arnot was invited to read a paper before the Royal Geographical Society in January 1889, which was printed in the 'Proceedings' of the Society together with a map of his routes and those of other African travellers, showing that he had traced the true course of the first part of the Zambesi river, and was the first to locate the sources of 'this great water highway'. He was then made a Fellow of the Society.

Arnot was fêted everywhere and even introduced to the Duchess of Teck and her daughter the Princess Mary, later to become Queen Mary, who together took him for a drive around Hyde Park, and listened to the stories of his travels. Arnot wrote to his mother, quite amazed at this, saying 'The Princess would have me drive off in her carriage with herself and another Princess, and asked about you and Dad and was so glad to see me, and would never forget me, and was so helped.'

Frederick Stanley Arnot was approached at this time by Wilson and Walter Fisher. He visited their homes, and met Harriet Fisher at Greenwich. Both men volunteered to return to Africa with him, as they had just been qualified as doctors. They had worked side by side at Guy's Hospital, and often had reached the top two places in their examinations. Sometimes one came first, sometimes the other. They now decided they were ready and anxious to give their lives to take the gospel of Jesus Christ to those who had never heard it in Africa, first by means of medical knowledge and work. They spoke to Arnot and he was enthusiastic. He had another interest in their company. Visiting Walter Fisher's home, he had fallen in love with Harriet, and shortly before he left England with a number of volunteers, he was married to her in 1889. Arnot and all the new missionaries were to go out in faith, depending only on God for help and believing that He would supply all their needs. Two great valedictory meetings were held, and it was arranged that the missionaries were to sail in two groups, the first arriving in Africa in May, headed by Arnot and his wife, the second in August, when the young doctor, Walter Fisher, was one of the number. But Wilson, bitterly disappointed and sad at saying farewell to his greatest friend, was not to be with them. After the necessary medical examination he had been told his health would under no circumstances be strong enough to survive the rigours of such a mission, and that he would be a liability. Pale and with set face, he fought his own battles for he had steadily refused to admit his early delicacy, and had lived in hospital in a spartan fashion. Now he felt he had failed his friends. Later he was to volunteer to go to China, and again be turned down on health grounds.

When he emerged from the disappointment of those days, he made a vow which he was faithfully to keep. From that moment on, his finest work, his utmost concern, would be given to every missionary who needed medical help in after years. It would be given free, and his life would be dedicated to healing those who could do the work from which he had been barred. Missionaries of every denomination, every outlook, and in any need whatsoever, never thereafter came to him for help in vain, and his cures of some were later to be called almost miraculous.

He went to see Walter off at the docks one summer day in 1889 and to wish him God speed. It was to be many years before they met again. Walter Fisher was to become an outstanding and loved figure in medicine in Africa, and his great achievement was again assessed only recently, when an American writer, Rotberg, wrote in 1965 of his work at Kalene Hill which was to become very well known as 'a major centre of curative medicine'.

Wilson turned sorrowfully back to the slums and fogs of London, to work among the poor in the crowded wards of Guy's Hospital. After qualifying, he had been chosen for a post of special responsibility. It was, he now thought, an answer to prayer. He had a special interest in the diseases of women and children, and he was asked by Mr Peter Horrocks, the obstetrician, to be his Resident Obstetric Assistant in the hospital. Peter Horrocks was one of the first men to perform successfully the operation of Caesarian section. He was always intensely careful and humane in all his work, and achieved remarkable success. His vivid blunt character, and his fondness for the young man he had chosen to help him, eased for Wilson the disappointment of seeing his friend go abroad to do alone the work that he had longed to do with him. Horrocks' calm commonsense acceptance of life taught him to relax and accept what was hard. Calmness was part of the very make-up of Horrocks who was a very keen mountaineer. He was often to tell the astonishing story of how he only just escaped death in Switzerland, when climbing roped to two guides. One fell and was killed, and Horrocks would have been also, had not the rope on which he was suspended been caught on a boulder. While he hung suspended against the cliff face, he calmly took his own pulse, and was relieved to find it steady. Such was his self-control in a moment of crisis.

Eventually Wilson turned his thoughts to his own future and discussed it with Horrocks, who advised him to apply for a certain vacant post at the Royal Hospital. He wrote a glowing testimonial for him, saying he had 'conspicuous ability', and alluding to him as his 'friend and pupil'. Wilson was surprised at the references many of the great men of Guy's Hospital gave him. Wrapped up in his work, intensely interested in his patients, he was largely unaware of his own potential. He posted off the testimonials and the photo and waited. After the interview, he was greatly surprised to receive a letter saying that his application was successful, and he was appointed Resident Medical Officer at the Royal Hospital for Women and Children in Waterloo Bridge Road in the same year as Walter, his friend, departed for Africa.

Wilson packed his bags, his books, purchased some new clothes, and set off, aged twenty-five. Now in a top hat and frock coat himself, and in a hired cab, he arrived at the gates of the 'Royal Waterloo' to begin a new period of his life.

It was about this time that the foundation of his whole existence had been shaken in another way. Thomas, his father, caught a chill walking back from the business on a wet night. He had been overworking, and was also concerned for Jennet his wife, who was far from well, and who now spent much of her life on a couch. The happy carefree girl in the large family of fourteen children in Lincolnshire had become over the years an almost beautiful woman. A daguerrotype shows her fine firm features, her slightly shadowed cheeks, and an expression of serenity yet sadness. She appears to sit lost in thought, almost as if she had some premonition of the future. It was Thomas whose chill developed swiftly into pneumonia and he died with horrifying suddenness, leaving his family stunned. He was still young in spirit and full of vitality; it seemed he could not be gone. Jennet was too unwell to cope with the grief. She became seriously ill, and died shortly after her husband.

It was now that the members of the family drew together, looked to each other for comfort, and turned to their father's God, who was so real, so powerful in their lives, that to take a step without his guidance was unthinkable.

It was Edith and Lucy who turned their thoughts to China, the last place where Victorian women might be expected to travel. To them it was quite simple, and was the culmination of much thought. Deeply affected by their father's faith, they had made it their own, had given their lives to God, and had waited for Him to reveal His plans. Now He was showing them the way. After training, they set out with other volunteers in the China Inland Mission to take up pioneering work among women in the interior, and to carry the gospel to those who, as they said, 'did not know our Lord'.

Wilson, with a heavy heart, saw them off, for China was another country to which he had considered going. It was saddening that his sisters were judged fit to go abroad and he was not. Lucy, the youngest of the family, was his favourite sister. She was the 'beautiful one', and he was happy with her because she was more gentle and gay than some of them, and had her mother's lively kindness. He felt he would miss her keenly. Standing on the dockside again, and waving to them as the great ship slowly moved away from the shore, he was full of grief. Perhaps he had some premonition that he would never see Lucy again. It seemed as if the family had broken up and now he was really alone. But he knew it would be a test of his faith, and he determined to face up to anything that happened to him as part of God's plan for him. Alone he left the docks and turned back to the hospital, for there were, he knew, many who desperately needed his care, and he believed that he had now been shown clearly and plainly that his work was first of all to be in London.

During his years at the Royal Waterloo Hospital, Wilson lived a life of ceaseless activity. Often he was up at night, directing and assisting in cases of difficult birth, or sitting beside small children with tuberculosis and wasting diseases or in delirium with high fever. Some of them he recalled later, and their merriment when they had good days as they shouted and laughed with each other in the children's wards, and often he knew there was no hope for them. He had little time for social life. He had heavy loads of responsibility and for each patient in his hospital he had an intense caring concern.

One morning he was awakened by an urgent messenger at his bedside. 'A message from Buckingham Palace, doctor', said the agitated bursar, shaking the tired young man. 'Her Royal Highness, the Princess Alexandra, wishes to visit the hospital this morning'. Wilson leaped out of bed aghast, as it dawned on him that he must himself escort her around the wards. He was totally unused to such functions. Quickly he put on his formal morning suit, and white gloves, and carrying his top hat, went to the front of the hospital to wait for the Royal party and to receive the wife of the heir to the throne. 'She was a very slender little lady,' he said afterwards, 'and she seemed like a beautifully made doll'. He found his Royal guest was pleased with the medical progress made even since he had been appointed the Resident Medical Officer, and he was relieved that he seemed able to cope properly with the occasion.

During these years he returned at regular intervals to Guy's Hospital, generally carrying a bunch of flowers. He had from student days admired one of the young lady nurses who became a ward sister. 'She was the only woman I ever wanted to marry', he said afterwards, but in this, as in other ways, he was being disciplined to severe disappointment. She was a convinced and devout Anglican, and came from a wealthy county family. She regarded his religion as narrow and odd, if not actually heretical. Yet she was drawn to the persistent young man, who never seemed to turn his thoughts elsewhere. Year after year he visited her at infrequent intervals and her answer to his proposal of marriage was always the same. It was no.

It never seems to have occurred to him to reconsider his own position. He was totally convinced that the rejection by the Brethren of the traditional structures of the Episcopal Church, and also of the organisations found in many dissenting sects was right, because only so he believed, could he worship God with freedom of conscience. Denominational disciplines were abandoned so that men could get back to grass roots and follow simply the practices of the early apostolic church. He was afraid of the formality of church life as he saw it. He wanted to worship with all believing men and join in the free celebration of the Lord's Supper, in a gathering where all men could exercise the gifts God had given to them. Cultured, having great interest in scientific knowledge gained in his already extensive medical work, he was still able to reject the tidal waves of doubt sweeping across the thought of the day because of the so-called conflict between science and religion. Always he found some explanation to deepen his fundamental rock-like belief. The Bible was his charter and guide, and in it he found all rules for life. Difficulties, he was totally sure, would always eventually yield in the face of faith, and then the vision of Christ would shine the more brightly. Nothing, then, would alter his convictions, but he grew heart-sick at the steady refusal of the one woman he loved to understand them. She, on her part, was totally convinced of the rightness of her own position. Influenced somewhat by the Tractarian tradition, which emphasised the mystic spirituality of the historic Church, she would have considered herself a traitor to let her beliefs go.

Wilson became lonely and the burden of his work grew heavier. One night as he walked through a London street, returning to the hospital, he was accosted by a prostitute. Under the street gas lamp, he looked sadly at the face which had traces of beauty and pathos, and he knew he was human. But like Christian in *Pilgrim's Progress* he believed there was one expedient for a man sorely tried. It was to flee temptation. He was so alone that he felt drawn to the solitary figure, but there was only one thing to do. He turned and ran through the night while his echoing footsteps mocked him, and the girl leaning against a doorway looked unbelievingly after him into the darkness.

After some years at the hospital he began to wonder where he was eventually meant to work. He believed God would lead him to the right place provided he was ready and waiting. In all his decisions he turned to the Bible. Day by day as he read, the words leaped to life as if they had been specially written for his need at that moment. He believed that, while the words properly referred to their own situation and context, yet they were the 'living Word', and gave a message and meaning to other times and other conditions when they were read by those who looked for definite guidance or solace.

At this moment a doctor friend in Bath wrote to tell him that there was a need in that city for more men in general practice, and he would greatly welcome Wilson as a near-by colleague. The Bible came out, and the young man pored over it, and as he read, the words of the psalmist leaped to his eyes: 'I will instruct thee and teach thee in the way which thou shalt go. I will guide thee with mine eye'. As he was to recount later, it was the message he needed. He made arrangements to leave his post in London which he was said to have filled with distinction, and took a house in Bath, in a residential area full of both middle-class houses and poor dwellings where the land sloped down to the canal. Two of his sisters kept house for him, and he put up a brass plate and waited. It was a tense anxious time. At last one morning a little servant girl rang the front door bell in great agitation as her mistress was ill. He set off to his first patient. His new life had begun.

Step by step the practice grew. When it was clearly established, he decided to go back once more to Guy's Hospital. It was to be a final proposal of marriage, and the answer must be Yes or No, he said. With a bouquet of roses he sent a letter saying it would be the last time he returned. A brief note was eventually handed to him. It is hard to imagine his feelings as he opened it and read, 'Let it be as you wish'. If the answer seems a little formal, even withdrawn, the outcome was at first to bring him happiness such as he had not easily imagined. He was alone no longer.

4

TWO CHILDREN

THE years that began so happily, eventually brought tragedy
to Wilson. He brought his wife home to the house in
Bath. Somehow, at last, they had settled their differences,
and her devout adherence to the Anglican Church, and his
to the Plymouth Brethren, were accepted by each. The
harmony between them seems to have been undisturbed.
He could discuss all the problems of his work with her, share
his hopes and anxieties. Her love for him was steady and
serene. Little tiny notes left for him in the house, if ever she
had to be out, were found years later still carefully preserved.
They were full of love and practical concern: 'Do not forget
to eat your lunch today!' read one, and there must have been
a smile on her face as she wrote, for she knew well how often
he became so totally immersed in the care of a very sick
patient that he forgot meals and forgot the time, for he was
concentrating deeply and intently on the one who needed his
care.

He travelled to his patients in a carriage drawn by a pair
of horses, a brougham in bad weather, a Victoria or open
carriage if fine and warm. Wearing a top hat and formal suit,
as did most doctors at the time, he must have looked quite a
distinguished figure,—and an unusual one. As the coachman
drove the horses around Bath, up and down the hills, into the
surrounding country, from patient to patient, Wilson
would read tirelessly, the latest medical text-books, or the

Greek New Testament, or he would strain his eyes to master the Scriptures in Hebrew, his mind voracious, the brain quick and alert, grasping at all medical knowledge, all Scriptural enlightenment. It was the study of the latter that affected the former. As the carriage swayed from side to side, and the horses trotted briskly along, the pale young doctor studied and thought, and committed every activity of the day to God.

In his work his brain was agile, leaping ahead of conventional treatments to new developments, to new scientific discoveries, and to the more skilful and effective blending of medicines. He became the despair of chemists, yet his courtesy was their delight. But his prescriptions were so detailed, often new and unheard of in his day, and had to be made up so meticulously, and the instructions were so minute and careful, and often lengthy, that no label was adequate in size to contain them. His patients, often in astonishing and unfavourable circumstances, prospered. But then, each one was 'committed to the Lord'. When they were gravely ill, he never let go, never gave up hope, never spared himself. People got used to the swift sound of the horses' hoofs during the darkness of night, to the footsteps passing at a run down the path into the carriage. No hour was too late, no trouble too great. He ran everywhere. Into the home, eager and happy, smiling, affectionate, full of tiny details of news; up and down the stairs; meals were often rushed because people needed him and were waiting; and he would be off again, into the carriage. He was tireless. As with many of his relatives, his unflagging energy made others fall back, almost daunted. The questioning mind never seemed to weary. Nothing was too much trouble. Travelling to London and Edinburgh to take the highest qualifications in medicine, he was also at this time studying, and working indefatigably, ceaselessly striving to perfect his medical knowledge. He already was MB, MRCS, LRCP, but in 1890 he took his MD at London and proceeded to take the MRCP of Edinburgh in 1900. He was becoming known as one of the finest physicians in the city.

Happiness came, and joy, when first one and then another baby daughter was born. The man who loved children now lavished his affection on his wife and his own babies, when he had any leisure to do so. Perhaps his joy was too concentrated. It was tragically short-lived. Seven years after his marriage, when his children were still babies, his wife fell ill with diabetes for which there was then no cure. His joy turned to the deepest sorrow. He watched his wife, to whom his devotion was total, slowly die. He had only been married for eight years when he was left alone, with two tiny motherless children, and a sense of irreparable loss. He nearly despaired for a time, and indeed were it not for the consolation of his unshakable faith, he might well have done so. But the children were left. The elder was so inconsolable for her mother that she seemed to be slipping away and in danger of going into a decline. In caring for her, he partly rallied, but the joy, the shared laughter, the serene happiness, had gone. He could not, even in later life, speak of those days without distress.

Another tragedy struck at the closely-knit family. He had said farewell to his sisters, Edith and Lucy, when they set out on their great mission and adventure to China. Often travelling great distances, wearing Chinese clothes, working among the people in arduous difficult conditions, evangelising, teaching, they lived a life of hardship and challenge. The gentle Victorian women had the courage of pioneers. Edith must, I think, have been the dominant one, but Lucy, the sweet-natured gentle sister, was of all the family closest to Wilson. Even in a photograph, the face glows with a kind of inner happiness. But Lucy contracted typhoid fever, and after a short illness died with the same almost shocking unexpectedness as her father.

To Edith, still in China, Wilson then turned in his distress, looking for someone to look after his motherless children, and run his household. Edith settled her affairs, gave up all her plans, and returned to him, and having given up all the work on which her heart was set, gave herself to her brother's children with the same concentrated concern as she had given to the women of China. For her the cost of altering her life was great, but she never spoke of it. Stoical, determined, she showed a tender loving side to the children. But those who did not know her sometimes found her forbidding, for she had a steely strength of character that could give an impression of severity.

The household was now in the hands of two very different people, both strong and unbending in character. They dominated the lives of others, and I believe were not even conscious of it. Wilson had become a man of inflexible will and determination. His sister had similar qualities. In this house two little girls lived out their childhood. They had no understanding mother to interpret their father's sometimes inexplicable character to them, or to sense instinctively their own needs and longings just because they were her own children. Their aunt immersed herself dutifully in their interests, and supervised their lessons with the help of a young cousin who came as a nursery governess.

Wilson's practice grew. He became an honorary consultant physician at the Bath hospitals. Sometimes he travelled to London to study the latest medical developments. Constantly he added to his already large medical library.

In keeping with his appointment as a consultant, he moved to Brock Street, whose tall and imposing Georgian houses linked the Circus and the Royal Crescent, two triumphs of eighteenth-century architecture. The Circus was a unique massive circle of houses, constructed in three separate and perfect curves or crescents, so astounding to the eyes of Tobias Smollett, the novelist and doctor, that he described it as being like the Colosseum in Rome turned inside out. The Royal Crescent, noble and majestic in cream-coloured stone, lay above the Victoria Park, and seemed to dominate the city which sloped away below and covered the gentle hills opposite. It was the area where successful and often distinguished professional men lived, many of them doctors and surgeons. Bath with its Spa waters was a centre for rheumatic patients. The air, often mild and warm, was considered beneficial for children and the elderly. Many visited the city for their health and came to the consulting-rooms in Brock Street.

Wilson worked night and day. Often he would sit beside seriously ill patients far into the small hours to help them and give them confidence, allowing them to relax into a health-giving sleep. Some of his patients became devoted to him. His care drew out their affection. One young woman always remembered the sympathy with which he told her that she must have an operation or die in middle life.

'I have never forgotten his sympathetic manner, his extreme gentleness, and the strong faith he put into me . . .', she said. She had a serious operation and lived to recall the time.

'When I said "Goodbye" to him, I told him that I could have gone to the guillotine with him', she said. Many years later that memory was still strong.

Once he had an unusual experience. It was perhaps the nearest approach to the miraculous in his work, and he told his sister about it, and later others in his family:

'I believe on one occasion God did speak to me in a special, almost miraculous way. Charles (the coachman) had

driven me some miles out of Bath to see a certain lady who
had been very ill. I found her almost recovered, and she
and her husband were exceedingly grateful for all I had
been able to do for them, and thanked me profusely. So I
left feeling very pleased at this. Considerably later, the
horses were nearing the city again, and I was extremely
hard-pressed for time, and was just planning my list of
visits. Suddenly, and totally unexpectedly, I felt as if I was
being told to turn back immediately to go and see Mrs S.
again, as it was a matter of great urgency. It was like an
insistent voice inside my head, and I could not get away
from it. In view of her great improvement it seemed
entirely nonsensical. But the feeling persisted, getting
stronger and stronger, that I must return. I made it a
matter for prayer therefore at once. I seemed to be told
again that I must indeed return. I told Charles to turn
the horses. He was amazed, for he knew how much work
we still had before us. But we retraced the road as quickly
as possible, I feeling somewhat foolish, and yet apprehensive of the reason. When we arrived at the house, we found
the husband standing anxiously on the front door-step,
almost wringing his hands. His amazement at seeing us
was mingled with extraordinary thankfulness. "Oh,
Doctor", he said, "how could you possible know? My
wife has suddenly been taken desperately ill. I think she
may be dying, and I have been earnestly praying for you
to return." I'm glad to say that simply because I arrived
in the nick of time I was able to save the lady's life, and she
made a full recovery.'

Some might have called it telepathy. To him it was a clear
and shining answer to prayer.

The two children growing up in this Edwardian home were
sensitive and alert. Their world was ruled by their aunt,

peopled with the 'servants', and over and above them all moved the figure of their father, of whom they saw comparatively little; he was the head of the household, austere perhaps, authoritarian, and yet always loving. He could, too, on occasion, cast off his responsibilities, and try and enter their games and interests. It was as if, briefly, he became a boy again. Then once more, his medical work would call, and he would be off, working long hours often until late at night. The children began to notice that he showed some unusual qualities. They heard their aunt remind him that two aged spinsters owed him something like thirty-one pounds and had written for their account. His reply was, 'Oh, dear, I hoped they'd forget it'. It was the greatest effort to him to allow his sister eventually to send a bill for two pounds. The children were to learn that all through his life he had the deepest dislike of sending out bills to anyone who might find it difficult to pay.

The second unusual thing about their father, and it made him so different from the fathers of their friends, was his practice of suddenly praying. Any problem, any difficulty facing the family was met with the response, 'Let us ask the Lord about this'. There and then, sometimes to the confusion of his children, sometimes to their embarrassment, he would kneel and speak to his 'Heavenly Father' simply and reverently as if he was talking to a real person in the room. It was difficult for the children to understand that this, in fact, was exactly what he was doing. His sense of the presence of his Master beside him in all his work, had a profound effect on some of his patients. His certainty of divine help, even if it were not mentioned—and he did not talk about it unless he was asked—gave them a feeling of confidence. One day the eight-year-old son of a prominent Bath citizen became gravely ill, with no prior warning, with a perforated appendix; Wilson was summoned, and within an hour the large bedroom had been transformed into an operating theatre, and four doctors including Wilson and the surgeon were fighting for his life. The mother, desperately anxious, walked up and down the hall for what seemed an eternity, and at last footsteps were heard on the stairs. The surgeon came down drawing on his gloves, and said briefly, unemotionally, 'Well, it's on the cards he may live'. The mother stood, very shocked. Wilson followed quietly, went up to her and took her hand, and said very gently, 'We have left him in the hands of God'. The mother was later to recount how those words lingered with her through all the long weary months of the child's slow recovery, and as she said, made all the difference. The child grew to be an outstanding doctor, well known for unique research work at home and abroad.

The difficulties that subsequently arose for Wilson's children may have in part stemmed from the fact that his apparently unquestioning faith was held in a period of history when there was a crisis of thought that had begun in England and abroad during his early childhood. Re-interpretations of Christian doctrine had been taking place in Germany as a result of the work of well-known scholars in Biblical criticism, which clearly seemed to cast doubt in the eyes of many on the infallibility of the Bible, and were therefore deeply shocking. By 1900 many had accepted the chief conclusions of the new thinkers. But evangelicals, a large number of nonconformists, some Catholics and most Roman Catholics still held that the Bible must be interpreted in its literal sense. At the beginning of the century, doubts were cast on the traditional doctrines of the person of Christ and the miracles in the gospels through the work of different theologians. In the ensuing debate, the 'Modernist Party' in the Church of England came into existence, and Charles Gore, Scholar of Oxford, who was to become successively Bishop of Worcester and Birmingham and had himself been

modernist in outlook, now demanded that some authorita-
tive statement should be made of what a loyal churchman
could believe, in order to halt the rising tide of unbelief in
Christian thought.

In the midst of these current controversies Wilson walked
undisturbed, glad because in his own faith, and in his
Christian group, he had found reality and certainty. To him
the words of the Bible lived. Nothing and no one could take
that from him. The differing beliefs, and the doubts of some
in the Anglican Church caused him to hold all the more
strongly to his own path. He hurled doubt from him. His
Bible told him all he wished to know for life. That was enough.
Yet he was a wide reader, studying Westcott, Handley
Moule, sermons by Spurgeon, the great Baptist, and works
by many of the evangelical thinkers. He had also deliberately made himself familiar with some Catholic and Roman
Catholic thought in order to be able to discuss Christian
belief with patients and friends of different outlook. While
holding rigidly to his own views, he never lightly dismissed
the sincere beliefs of others. Nevertheless, he was totally convinced of the rightness of his thought. It was so clear. For
him 'The Truth' was a shining reality, and the blindness, as
he regarded it, of scholars and thinkers to appreciate this, had
one result only, to make him sad for all they missed of joy
and certainty in knowing his Lord. In this manner the
character of their father was a strong influence in the children's lives. They were made to follow the same religious
routines as he and his aunt had been taught in their childhood.

In the house itself, life was entirely different from life
today. Two worlds were encompassed in one, that 'below
stairs' where the servants lived in rather dark rooms looking
out into areas below street level, fenced off from the street
above by iron railings; and that on the ground floor where

the consulting-rooms and dining-room were, and upstairs where the family lived. The children were fond of some of the different maids who worked there over the years, and yet there was always the conscious knowledge that their position made them different—an attitude which is for the most part alien today. Their father regarded every soul as a child of God, and he had a positive alert concern for every person in his household. But he was not, I think, conscious of any lack of equity between his life and that of the women in the kitchens. He saw it all as part of a pattern of patriarchal living, where each person had his 'station', and it was equally important to serve God in the kitchen as in the consulting-rooms. He was the Master of the household, alluded to as such, and was a figure to be obeyed and to be looked up to with respect. The maids called the children 'Miss D' and 'Miss M', and they even called Crusoe the cat 'Master Crusoe'! Whether this peculiar fact was due to a little humour on their part, or whether on the children's who may have spoken of him as if he was another human member of the family above stairs, it is hard to tell. There is, however, a rather sad picture, one of the children later recalled, of the widower, dining quite alone in his dignified dining-room when they were sick upstairs and their aunt was beside them; the parlourmaid waited on him at the table, and he always had a chair placed beside him for 'Master Crusoe', who at such times was his only companion at meals.

The life of the children was comfortable physically, and secure. It was the maids who each day placed hip baths for the family in front of coal fires in the bedrooms, and carried brown lidded enamel cans of water up the long flights of stairs from the kitchens, for there was initially no bathroom in the great house. They were given many good books to read by relatives and patients, including the classics, children's story books by E. Nesbit, Mrs Molesworth, Francis

Hodgson Burnett and many others; and beautiful toys. There was the large rocking-horse, beautiful dolls' tea-sets, and wickerwork dolls' carriages to push outdoors. With their governess, a cousin, they were encouraged to work hard at lessons and to achieve the highest possible standards. Nothing slipshod or untidy would do. They were watched over, guided, and dutifully cared for. But shut away in the upstairs nursery, they lacked one of the most important things in life, the spontaneous warmth and relaxed happiness of their mother's love. One of the children was, I surmise, less sure of herself than the other, who had a strong passionate character and who lived every minute intensely, full of endless energy and often frustration. They were totally unlike each other in outlook, except that, when they ultimately went to the High School, they both worked with unusual concentration, one needing to take her work slowly and deliberately, the other forging ahead, determined always to reach the top at everything she could, gaining prizes, putting the same concentrated vigour into her work as her father, in a different manner, put into his. The other, I believe, found her problems harder to face. Conscious, I am sure, of loneliness, of longing for her mother, there is a certain sadness of expression and wistfulness in some of her early photographs, while her sister looks more determined.

Small events stood out like beacons in their mind. There was the great excitement of the purchase of the new invention, a motor car. The doctor friend who had first urged their father to come to Bath, bought the first car in the city. Wilson promptly bought the second. Charles the coachman said it would never be the same as the 'osses'. But in fact master and man both enjoyed the new and exciting vehicle so much that they took turns to drive it. One day the new car skidded, and Charles, in great alarm, flung his arms around his master's waist, wailing 'Oh, sir, Oh, sir:' But Wilson was exhilarated with his new machine, and nothing marred his pleasure. On Sundays the car was never used. Charles had to have his day of rest, and Wilson, except in grave cases of emergency, bicycled to his patients on a large black and gold Sunbeam model.

Then there was the excitement of holidays with their aunts, and Uncle Harry and Aunt Maggie, Wilson's sister, whose lively happiness brought a breath of exhilaration into their lives. Her marriage to a cousin, a prosperous young banker, and her departure from the ranks of the Brethren, had brought her freedom and serenity. But she was still close to her sisters. So all together the great family journeyed to the seaside, just as they had as children with their father. One of my sisters vividly described the mountain of luggage packed for the holidays by their Aunt Edith:

'When we went on our summer holiday immense quantities of luggage accompanied us—huge domed trunks, our large circular tent and accompanying paraphernalia of pegs and mallet etc., our nursery bath completely filled with things and then covered over with hessian which Aunt E. sewed with a bent packing needle, such as you might use for sewing up a turkey after you'd stuffed it. To transport this mountain of luggage, W. Tall's luggage cart was summoned. . . .

'I remember bathing boxes, with little steps down from the door, so that you could step straight into the sea. Aunt E. had a navy blue bathing dress, with legs down below the knee, and a skirt (all edged with white braid); the skirt always floated up around her and lay on the surface of the sea, and never seemed to get waterlogged and sink.'

TWO CHILDREN ON HOLIDAY

They are with their aunts and Uncle Harry. Aunt Edith is in the back row, end R. Aunt Annie is seated on the grass R, beside the children.

Here in this small photo the children sit in front of a family group, taken on one of the holidays. This Edwardian family somehow reminds me of a solid phalanx facing the foe. Yet I know that behind those faces emotions were to run deep and poignant. It is difficult to get a clear picture of those days, and to understand all that eventually happened. No words can do more than suggest a situation and guess what might have been cause and effect. My two sisters—they are the children pictured in the front—have occasionally re- counted some of their recollections. Both, I would guess, have let the days lie buried in their memories, and can only find it sad, in part, to recall them.

Wilson and his sisters remained united in a bond that was unbreakable. In spite of differing characters, outlook and work, they were to come together again and again over the years, as if drawn by a magnet. If at times they could quarrel, argue or disagree, it was only the superficial mood of a moment. It was typical that they should be pictured here all together at the seaside, for they always seemed to do things in a crowd, and to be happy when they acted in unison.

Whenever the father had to go away from his children, he wrote them loving little letters, sadly, I think, trying to fill the rôle of both father and mother. His letters were spon- taneous, and always full of interest at everything he noticed around him. Like his own father, he was passionately fond of trains, studying all information about railways, the different models of engines, and the mileage per hour. Often, as here, he wrote to them as he sat in the train:

'I am in one of those great big new carriages, with a cor- ridor, and a handle to turn on the steam to make the carriage either COLD or HOT, It is lit with incandescent gas and a dear little thimble-shaped mantle upside down which gives a beautiful light, and two green tassels at the side of the lamp to pull the light up, or put it out. The floor has linoleum on it, and the door into the corridor slides to and fro if you want to move it. . . . Both my companions slumber quietly. The little dog thinks we are going too fast.'

When his sister Alice was seriously ill in South Africa, and he made the journey of a lifetime to be with her for a month, he wrote to tell them about everything he found of interest on his journey. His letters were full of lively detail. He told them of the flying fish, the wonders of the scenery, the luxurious morning bath in a new-fangled bathroom with a 'lovely big bath enamelled smooth'; and he described Lord Methuen's horses travelling out to the Cape in padded boxes tied to iron railings on deck; he shows his acute pleasure at being specially allowed with another passenger to go into the engine-rooms and the stoke-holes. But whenever he wrote to his children, it is clear he realised acutely their lack of the mother to whom he had been so wholly devoted, and his affection flows out:

'May you, each, be one of the Lord Jesus Christ's little lambs, so very near to his loving heart; may you both know Him, the Good Shepherd who laid down his life for you, as your very own Saviour.'

Was it then his zeal for their souls' welfare, his concern, so concentrated, that in the end brought about something like another tragedy for him? In the months and years of their childhood and early adolescence, the children longed for the more normal church of their mother, which they attended from time to time when taken to the parish church by one of the aunts. They thirsted ardently and deeply for beauty in religion, for they had just as strong spiritual instincts as their father; they were deprived of music in the meetings of the Brethren, and both were intensely musical.

Eventually they began steadily to turn away from their father's puritan faith which apparently spoke so little to them, and never, it seemed, filled their real needs.

It was the Sunday routines that bred in two restless children such a deep resentment. It was understandable. They knew that their mother had been a staunch member of the Church of England which their friends all attended. To find that not only could they not attend her church, and be like other people, but that their father considered its doctrines wrong, created a violent clash of loyalites. Their mother's memory was, no doubt, kept alive for them in the words of relatives. When, Sunday by Sunday, they sat in dull surroundings in a plain hall, on hard bare seats, listening to extempore prayers often of great length, and Bible readings and exhortations that utterly failed to captivate their eager minds, their spirits rebelled.

They also began to resent Wednesdays, the day the missionaries came to lunch. True to his vow, their father gave up a large part of his time to give free treatment to all missionaries needing his medical care. Every Wednesday one or two came to lunch. The conversation, 'over the roast beef or lamb' as one described it, offended their reticence or sensitivity, for their father would often ask the guests to recount how they first were 'brought to the Lord'. He seemed quite unaware of their feelings; for him, living in an almost biblical atmosphere, permeated by the words of Scripture, it was the most natural thing in the world for true Christians to recount. Was not this the most important experience of life, and a matter for rejoicing? Was it not at the table, over a meal, that the disciples, who had walked the Emmaus road with Christ, suddenly recognised him? Why not speak of it, then, at a shared meal?

I can believe that the spiritual questioning was an agonizing experience to the two girls as they grew older. Adolescent emotions can be very tender, very delicate. For the girls, faith must die if it had to be thus exposed and examined. It was, therefore, perhaps inevitable that slowly, surely, and irrevocably they turned from their father's way of life. Helped by the sympathetic rector of the parish, and no doubt by one of the aunts, they were prepared for confirmation, and eventually left their father's meeting hall for ever. This step was to be their emancipation, and both embraced their mother's church as ardently as their father stood in undeviating loyalty to his place of worship. Determined, uncompromising, they were, but also, I believe, hurt. I have no doubt that over the years they had suffered. They had been made different from their friends, had been denied the traditional beauty of the liturgical services, and the mystical element in Christianity.

It was now that their father endured a feeling of deep grief. He saw his hopes shattered. He believed himself to be a failure, for in his view he had utterly failed to pass on to his children the beauty of his Lord to Whom his whole life was given. He had, in some way, embarrassed his children. Trying to reach them, intensely anxious to help them understand great eternal truths, he had, in a sense, driven them from him. Perhaps their mother could have interpreted to them their father's character, for she had understood him so well. But because she was not there, father and children, in the words of Edmund Gosse brilliantly describing a not dissimilar and poignant relationship with his own father, began to walk 'in opposite hemispheres of the soul'.

Shortly after this, the whole world altered tragically. The cataclysmic onslaught of the German armies in 1914 at the beginning of the first world war brought Wilson ceaseless work. Turned down for the Army on grounds of age, he was made consultant physician to the Bath War Hospital. In addition, he took over no fewer than five practices of doctors who went to the front. These he was to hand back intact, which was almost a superhuman achievement. Working night and day, for the casualty lists were appalling, he grew greyer and graver, and I think more deeply lonely.

In his work he prospered. At about this time he moved his household to a great house in the Circus. I think it was his heart which was empty. It was during the war that an event occurred which was to change not only his whole life, but that of his household. He met and proposed to the young headmistress of a public school in Bath. It was a step that brought grief to his sister Edith. Recalled from China where her pioneering work had been so fascinating to her, she had given up everything to come to look after her brother's motherless children, and had put all personal plans aside. Now, it appeared, she would no longer be needed, and she had no home. One of my sisters discovered her weeping bitterly. She had looked on the children as her own, and had now to give them up.

Looking back in imagination, I can only dimly guess at her grief, at the determination of my father, and at the clash of character that must have ensued. I am full of pity for everyone concerned. They acted with motives that were honourable. Their vision and understanding may have been limited, but they were trapped in a situation that was impossible to remedy, and which created different and violent, even if suppressed, emotions.

I can picture that once Wilson's mind was made up, it would not be altered. I can believe that, as he told me years later, he felt he had asked too much of his sister, and hoped she would now enjoy her freedom before it was too late. That she did not now want it, never occurred to him. He undoubtedly wanted a wife. For he was a warm-hearted, affectionate man. Moreover, he was drawn to this young academic woman, attractive to look at, a London vicar's daughter, who had won every scholarship open to her, and had taken Mathematics at a college which was later to become part of the University of London. She had risen steadily, and in a short time, to the top of her profession. He had met her at the school while attending some of the girls, for he was the Medical Officer.

The marriage took place during the war. Edith packed her belongings and returned to London to be in charge of a missionary training home.

A year later, to the joy of the man who loved children, a third daughter was born, the last to whom he might commit the imperishable truths of his faith.

I was that child, born in his middle life, an intruder, you might say, in his family, born in time of war.

ANNE

5

ANNE

My home was a gentle fortress. We looked out; but not many people really penetrated into the heart of it or knew the manner of our lives. The child in this studio portrait who looks so happy and confident grew up in a world enclosed, where she watched and waited for life and became slowly aware of the interplay of characters around her. She seems a stranger to me now, but once I knew her well enough, for I am facing myself. I must have been about four years old.

What memories draw me back to the great house through whose quiet rooms I wandered in those days? Two sounds call me; I can hear them yet. The bells of the Abbey ring through my mind, just as they did long ago when I heard them swinging and echoing across the sky, mellow and plaintive on a still summer evening; or tossed in a jangling clamour, now near, now far, by the stormy west wind as it buffeted the old house on a winter's evening. And like a dissonant recurring theme, the harsh restless cry of the rooks flying to their nests in the great plane-trees outside the nursery windows brought wild echoes from distant wind-blown spaces. I watched the birds rise and fall in the turbulent air high above the roof-tops.

Now I am running—back down the years, and the autumn wind is blowing a cloud of brown curling leaves around my small and gaitered legs; running through the park and away from my nurse, down Brock Street, faster and faster, and I

75

am laughing for I have left her behind. At last I come to the great dignified houses in the Circus and at one of the tall front doors I stand on tiptoe to reach the fluted brass door-knocker which I can hardly lift, so I ring on the polished bell. I seem to wait so long there that I peer through the brass letter-box into the long hall inside, watching the shiny linoleum for the sight of approaching black-shoed feet, and I hop up and down impatiently. Footsteps are heard at last, and I can just see the black stockings and white apron of the parlourmaid come into sight. She has had quite a long way to come from the basement kitchens. Slowly, at last, the door opens and I go in. I am at home.

Here I was born when my father was middle-aged and my two sisters were nearly grown up. The arrival of a baby in that ordered solemn house must have shaken its routine and disturbed the family. One of my sisters gave up her room and retreated to the attics, which seems hard; but by the time a nurse was installed, together with all the paraphernalia connected with the bringing up of a child in a professional house in 1916, she may have been glad to get out of the way, and in any case I had usurped much space. A gigantic pram now stood in the hall—rather oddly in a senior consultant's house; and my academic mother, often immersed in educational committees, and surrounded by books and embroidery, may well have gazed at me a little questioningly, I think.

My first memory dates back to that pram. I remember a garden where the sun-baked lawns lay precisely clipped, edged by flower-beds full of brilliant colour, and the old stone house stood mellow in the afternoon sunshine. Suddenly two small dogs snarling and snapping jumped onto the pram, threatening some intruder. One then turned on the other, and in that instant conscious memory split violently open, never entirely to close again. The moment of terror was etched for ever on my mind, buried there, and with it the picture of a dark blue pram rug with scalloped edges clutched wildly in shaking hands. Into that scene there swiftly came a reassuring figure. The dogs were lifted down, and, shocked and frightened, I was lifted up into strong comforting arms, and the one who would be for many years the dominating figure in my life took up his position on the stage where the drama of life began to unfold. At this moment I was first consciously aware of my father.

Life in the nursery was a little like being on an island, far from the stir and movement of the house downstairs. I was cared for by my nurse, who ceaselessly watched over my every movement, and concerned herself with my welfare. I awoke to the soft creaking of her black shoes as she moved around the room. The gas fire popped as it was lit, and hissed quietly and comfortingly, and as the little clock on the mantelpiece chimed seven, my day began.

It started with a positively ritual washing. Hot water, brought up from the basement kitchens in large brown cans with lids, was carried in by the housemaid. My nurse poured it into the flowered basin on the washstand, and I had to stand, shivering a little in a large white bath towel, while I endured her relentless attack with the face flannel as she lavished her care on my cleanliness. When I was dressed, my hair was brushed until it was glossy enough to satisfy her. As she pulled out the tangles she used to hiss through her teeth, as if to calm a restless little foal, 'Stand still now for mercy's sake', while I jigged and jerked to be free.

In early life the day settled down to a space on a shiny white American cloth placed on the nursery table where I was given breakfast, while my nurse watched to see I finished all the glutinous porridge, and then spooned a boiled egg out of its shell onto a saucer, sprinkled it with salt, and cut up fingers of bread and butter for me to dip into it. Then she would sit back, arms folded across her chest, creasing a little the top of the white starched apron, which creaked softly when she moved.

At last I was able to wriggle down from the cane-seated chair, the bib was untied, my face was washed again a little more briefly, and I was allowed the first freedom of the day, to go downstairs and visit my parents having their breakfast in quiet state in the lofty dining-room four flights of stairs below. Going downstairs meant escape, adventure, a breath of real life, instead of the cloistered security of the nursery. The smell of bacon floated tantalisingly up as I gripped the dark mahogany banister rail, and hopped down two stairs at a time, until I landed up in the high-ceilinged hall, and slowly turned the smooth round knob of the dining-room door.

Sitting at one end of the large table behind the gleaming silver teapot and hot-water jug, my mother always gazed up and smiled; sometimes the blue eyes were a little abstracted as if her thoughts were far away, and I was rather an unexpected addition to that house full of adults. Often immaculately dressed in some soft shade of blue, she had wavy auburn hair curved softly back into a graceful bun.

At the other end of the table sat my father. He was obviously older than my mother, although being thin, quick-moving and intensely active, he gave the impression of being younger than he was. His greying hair framed a pale face and his eyes were steady and penetrating. He looked at me each morning with the same expression, thoughtful, direct and calm. Then suddenly the composure would be relaxed, the solemnity banished, and the warm rather teasing smile would change his whole appearance. His rather grave appearance could often melt suddenly, disconcertingly, so that a sudden eruption of laughter would seize him.

I always went to my father first, and stood expectantly at the corner of the table, covered with the glossy linen cloth, laundered to gleaming whiteness. Looking at me with a penetrating glance, he would say:

'Can there be something you want?'

'Yes, my toast.'

'Hasn't Nurse given you any breakfast this morning?'

'Yes, but I want your corners.'

Taking up a knife and fork with the motions of a surgeon about to operate—indeed he had done a great deal of surgery in early days—he would neatly and precisely cut off geometrically accurate corners from the triangular pieces of toast in the silver rack, spread them with butter and hand them to me, one by one. Somehow no other toast ever tasted as good as this, and no day would be complete without this strange little ritual.

Often my father put an arm around me before he left the breakfast table, and tried to make me say after him two or three verses of a psalm, so that I could form the habit of carrying the living word of God in my mind. I was not a very apt pupil. I would be looking out into the garden, beguiled by the soft cloud of cherry blossom in the sunlight, or watching the first green as the massive chestnut tree burst into leaf. Yet even now after many years have passed, I can hear him saying, 'Can you say these words after me?' I find myself then, listening again to his gentle compelling voice as he spoke the first words that I ever learned: 'The Lord is my Shepherd, I shall not want.'

The afternoons were occasions for another activity, a walk in 'the fresh air'. From the upstairs regions of the houses around us the children emerged at 2.30. The front doors would open, almost ceremoniously, and prams and pushchairs were wheeled out by nannies in uniform, their hair shrouded in flowing veils, followed by clusters of older children on scooters or 'fairy' bicycles, or perhaps with wooden hoops. The cavalcades all converged on the Victoria

Park, moving in a measured progress. Here in summer the nannies gathered together on the seats to gossip, while the children, free for a brief time, raced up and down the footpaths and played elaborate games among the trees and shrubs dotted over the sloping grass lawns.

Brought here each afternoon first by my nurse, and later by a governess, I gazed a little enviously at the other children who all seemed to have brothers or sisters or friends, while I, years younger than the other members of my family, was always solitary. Sometimes, rather timorously, I joined in a game of hide and seek, lying flat on the grass to hide behind a gigantic stone urn that adorned the formally clipped grass near the bandstand. But quite often I was forgotten, and there was nothing else to do but to creep away into the shrubbery and peer over the wall at the distant world outside, at the gasworks in the distance, and the smoking factory chimneys near the canal half a mile away. I used to watch the shifting patterns of sunlight on the allotments where old men bent and straightened their backs, and planted potatoes and cabbages; they were oblivious of the silent watcher, peeping at them through the shiny aggressive smooth laurel leaves that felt like a cold and chilly caress on the cheeks as one pushed past.

Summer had its own delights, when around the bandstand all the deck chairs appeared, and red-coated bandsmen entertained the leisured ladies of Bath with light music. The military conductor, bowing and twirling his baton, would raise his white-gloved hand, and the sound would burst forth and echo with haunting gaiety among the trees, and linger on the warm summer air, reaching in muted distant notes the great houses standing serene, impassive, in the sunshine.

In winter, the nursery was my domain, full of treasures: the family of tiny china mice on the mantelpiece; the little glass-fronted cupboard wherein my father encouraged me to put strange fossils, pebbles, shells, feathers, birds' eggs, picked up on country walks, which was called my museum; the large white toy-cupboard; and best of all the big wooden table covered with a blue serge table-cloth. Within these walls imaginary worlds could be conjured up, for which the 'props' were of the simplest. With much heaving and pushing, the large wooden table was turned upside-down, and a boat was instantly ready to sail away across foreign oceans. It even had two decks, because the bottom of the big table drawer formed the upper one, and standing on this I gazed out at far horizons. The legs were mast, wheel and funnel. If the weather was threatening, then the table-cloth could be draped across the upturned legs to form a sort of awning or covered deck. Before a voyage, the ship was loaded with all sorts of necessary articles, a toy oven, a telescope, a torch, and with my teddy bear for companion, I would huddle down on the lower deck as we breasted the mounting waves.

Then perhaps a desert island loomed before us, and soon the table became a cave, a shelter, a secret hiding-place from the lashing of the tempestuous storm, dark, womb-like, and cosy. Teddy and I lay down together, my nose buried in his soft fur.

Life in those early days was entirely devoid of outside stimulus such as children have today, but within the house there was a wealth of material on which a child might feed the imagination. A number of Victorian pictures still remained on the lofty walls, an inheritance of past years. Around these my wandering mind built stories and reflections. Worlds unseen opened up, into which one could happily slip away. There was a massive nobility about certain Victorian art. It reproduced scenes photographically and in faithful detail. Objects appeared much as they did to the naked eye.

In the large consulting-room in the front of the house,

there hung a picture which to me as a small girl, perhaps five or six years old, seemed the ideal representation of all that my father was and did. It really caused me emotion to look at it, although what the emotion was, it is hard to define. It was bound up with my early relationship with my father, who seemed so benign, so god-like, whose life was spent in bringing healing and comfort to others. The picture, one of my favourites, was called 'The Doctor'. It showed a very sick child lying across two chairs—a makeshift bed—in a poor cottage home. The haggard and anxious father, labourer's shirt open at the neck, stood in the background. The weeping mother seated at a table, head buried on arm, was an epitome of grief. But sitting beside the apparently unconscious child a figure sat, leaning forward, chin on hand, watching with compassionate and intense concentration; a figure from whom nobility and caring love shone out. Just as I was full of admiring love for my father, so I grew to love that doctor. His face was full of tenderness for the sick child; and yet the anxiety just hinted at in the intent look, seemed tempered to the quiet acceptance of his agonising responsibility in holding in his hand at that moment the fate, the life or death of a child, which might depend largely on his skill. It was a face from which true goodness shone out, and I decided he must be a man of God, for was not that what my father was?

So the doctor became a hero in my childish mind, a person to be copied, and I applied myself to this task. Opportunity was not unlimited, but I enlisted the help of my dolls. I never really liked dolls. They were static lifeless things. But at least they could serve a useful purpose if they were sick, and now they became constantly ailing. The nursery became a hospital, and the routine of the stethoscope, temperature-taking and anxious watching over the patients took up most of my time. Now and then my father was summoned for a consultation. His brisk quick step would be heard ascending the stairs. He entered the room without the flicker of a smile, asked the condition of the patients that day, then carefully examined them, placing his stethoscope to their hard and shiny chests. Gravely he pronounced their condition serious, but not without hope if the right medicaments were carefully administered. He bowed politely to me when the consultation was over, and with a lurking smile said: 'I expect you to take the utmost care, nurse.'

When he had time to think about it, my father sensed I was lonely. Perhaps he remembered the warmth and bustle and the arguments in that old nursery in Blackheath, so full of children that it must often have seemed to be bursting at the seams. For sometimes after a heavy day's work he came into the room, and put an arm around my shoulder as I sat surrounded by toys in some imaginary adventure.

'Get out the draughts board', he used to say, 'we must have a game together.'

So we sat solemnly opposite each other, the child and the middle-aged father talking easily and affectionately. Often he was full of high spirits, teasing and joking, with a sort of carefree gaiety, as if he himself was young. Then the mood would change, and standing up he would gaze down at me gravely, almost sadly: 'Darling, I long for you to know the Lord. It is so happy to belong to Him'. I was sure he must be right, because in my childish mind he knew so much more than anyone else.

How happy then it was to feel safe, secure in his love, and to endure no conflict of the spirit.

MY MOTHER AND I

6

MY MOTHER

THERE are so few photos of my mother. She never posed to
have her likeness taken, for she was always looking for
pictures to make of other places and people. Here in the
album is a snapshot taken when she held me as a baby. I
believe she was happy then. It was taken during the first
world war.

She is the background to all my first memories, the one
who softened my path with my father, who helped me
through those first years at school, encouraging happiness
wherever it could be found. Nothing then could have
indicated to me that she had sternly disciplined herself, as I
believe, to accept the limitations of the life she entered upon
with my father. Nor could I know that when she married she
cut adrift from her moorings, and headed out on an uncharted sea, away from family, friends, and from all that had
made her.

My first clear memories of her are connected with early
school days. School was a happy place as she described it to
me, and I began my days at the High School in the sure
belief that here I would learn a thousand wonderful things.
I remember making a sort of intoxicated progress into gaiety,
breathless with excitement at playing in some little percus-
sion band on the triangle. I longed for the tambourine but
did not know how to fight to get it first. I sat enthralled on a
tiny cane chair, lost in an ecstasy of tinkling sound. I jumped

85

and climbed and bounded along benches in the gymnasium, sang odd little songs at music lessons, and learned to step delicately to tiny dance tunes. We spent happy hours pouring water from one jug to another to learn to measure, or gathering and counting little spiked chestnuts in their cases to teach us numbering. I do not think we learned very much, but the days passed swiftly and in sunshine.

The mistresses were gigantic figures of authority in my tiny world. I see them as clearly as if it was yesterday. An angular and genteel lady ruled over us in the junior school. Her face was pale and thin, and she had wild wispy hair forever escaping from a collapsing bun; as she passed from one desk to another, an errant hairpin would regularly tinkle to the floor. She wore silky shapeless jumpers that disguised any figure she may have had; but my eyes were always riveted by the long necklace of large red stones—rubies as I always imagined in my childish mind—that swung forward and were apt to hit me when she bent down to correct my feeble efforts at arithmetic. When agitated, or admonishing us, or in any way under stress, a not infrequent occurrence, she distractedly wound her pale long slender hands in and out of the necklace, while she enunciated emphatic instructions in a clear and lady-like voice.

The gym mistress was a masculine vigorous woman with short plainly bobbed hair, a severe fringe and a most commanding manner. She was ruthless in expecting the best of us, nothing weak or slipshod in movement or exercise would do. We were held up to exposure and ridicule if we failed, and we feared her sarcasm. Praise was rare but when it came, treasured. Absent-minded, a little curious, and apt to be carried away by my own thoughts, I was sometimes in dire trouble through failing to listen to her instructions. I was tapped severely on the head, and left chastened and subdued as I heard the stern rebuke 'Of all silly little people . . .'.

I had been at school rather over a year when I discovered, to my astonishment, that in these surroundings I was 'different' from my friends. My mother, having given up a private life of her own, retained her connection with public educational work; this became one of her chief outlets, perhaps the one in which she could work most freely and naturally, and here she made a notable contribution to the life of the city. From time to time she arrived in the hall of my school to be received with obvious pleasure and deference by that tall imposing figure, the Headmistress, of whom I was much in awe. It emerged that my mother was Vice-Chairman of the Governors, having only refused to be Chairman on my account. At first I basked rather smugly in her glory. But later I began to regret the whole thing.

She was in great demand as a speaker on many platforms. This, oddly, was a nightmare to her, and she often became physically ill beforehand. This strange situation taught me, over the ensuing years, much about my mother. Deeply sensitive, she looked at life with a courage that had only been won with difficulty. In spite of the positions of authority she had held so young, she sometimes seemed to me to show an inner fearfulness, not I believe apparent to outsiders, which as a child I could not understand, but of which I was conscious, so that from time to time I felt it was my task to encourage her, to pretend that I was bold and daring, whereas in fact the opposite was the case, and I am sure she was never for a moment deceived.

It became, however, something of an ordeal for me to have my own mother constantly paraded in the public eye on educational platforms, and exposed before the critical eyes of my companions. It seemed to fall monotonously to her lot to propose the vote of thanks to distinguished speakers at the High School prize-giving. I never won a prize until nearly the end of my undistinguished school career, and it was a little awe-inspiring, even in those first school days, to realise the heights of scholarship to which she had attained in her time. But sensing even then her nervousness, I found it deeply embarrassing to listen to her speaking on such occasions.

At about this time my mother was ever hopeful that I should reveal some unexpected talent. It was this that led to the disastrous experiment of sending me to learn the piano with a distinguished elderly friend of hers, a Doctor of Music, whom she had known in university days. Saturday mornings became a dreadful ordeal as it became apparent that I was untalented. How unfortunate in a home where it was constantly impressed on me that my older sisters had 'perfect pitch'! My lamentable and fumbling efforts at the keyboard, as I sat paralysed under the glare of the Mus. Doc. as I privately called her, became a nightmare. It was not, however, my character of which she disapproved. When I entered the room, she always began to sing, 'O, ruddier than the cherry, O kidling blithe and merry!'. 'That's my picture of you', she announced as I froze onto the piano stool, feeling pale and totally devoid of merriment. After some months, she asked my mother to remove me from her presence. My 'blithe and merry' qualities were obviously not enough.

But work was forgotten and inadequacies left behind when we slipped away to a private life of our own on Saturdays. It was the time when we could forget the stresses and strains of life at home, its rules and routines. Our pleasures were simple, our hearts were light and carefree, or so it seemed to me. I do not know what inner anxieties my mother hid from me. She seemed gay and at peace as we went through the Georgian streets to the shopping centre, down Milsom Street with its expensive luxurious shops, window-gazing. We bought nothing in that area, but went at eleven o'clock to Theobald's the Coffee Shop a little farther on. As we went through the glass doors, the smell of freshly roasting coffee hung on the air, which was filled with a comfortable whirring sound as the machines turned the clattering beans over the heat. There were small tables with dark green tiled tops and here in a corner we sat cosily, and sooner or later someone my mother knew would arrive, and over the steaming coffee she would exchange news and comments on the affairs of the day. As I sat there sipping my 'coffee-dash', I listened to many people pour out their problems, worries and anxieties to her. I never once heard her mention her own. She was an excellent listener, sympathetic, practical in advice, resolute in encouragement. She had a wholesome fearless attitude to life, tempered by her acceptance of its difficulties, and an unflagging interest in people and places. She never on these occasions discussed religion. Reticent and sensitive, she did not easily speak of her faith, for which I was privately thankful, although, if called in question, I know she would have staunchly defended it. When coffee was over, and shopping finished, she often took me to various places of interest. Sometimes we pushed our way through the heavy revolving glass doors of the Pump Room and she took me to sit beside the fountain where mob-capped ladies handed out glasses of the sulphurous-tasting waters to the rheumatic or to the curious. A small orchestra played lively tunes, and old ladies nodded and tapped their toes. I once saw an old gentleman of aristocratic appearance, with great aquiline nose and furrowed autocratic face, seated in a high-backed armchair. This was a son of Queen Victoria, the old Duke of Connaught who visited the city from time to time. It seemed to be a city of the elderly, and wealthy.

Occasionally we descended the winding broad staircase to the Roman Baths beneath the Pump Room where the dark green waters were steaming gently all the time in the Great Bath. Here huge goldfish would leap to the surface of the water for crumbs thrown by visitors, and we trod the same worn paving-stones as the Roman aristocracy, sandalled or barefoot, had walked centuries before.

As we walked through the city together, our conversation was easy, even gay. My mother's humour asserted itself. 'What a voice!', she sometimes said, after listening to some pompous or affected character in a shop or the café. And she would mimic the offending tones, and laugh at the conceits of man.

It was she who first fostered in me a love of literature, reading aloud to me on winter evenings after school, while I laboriously and crudely knitted my first scarf. Into that knitting went the undying memory of *The Tale of Two Cities*, Dickens' immortal tale of the French Revolution; I saw the pathetic figure of Dr Manette returning to his cobbler's bench when trouble overwhelmed him; the coarse and violent figures who yelled at the French aristocrats on their way to the guillotine in Paris; and the sinister figure of Madame Defarge, knitting, knitting, her dreadful purpose unrevealed. Drama and the cosy flicker and glow of the large fire in the beautiful drawing-room hearth, mingled inextricably in my mind. The flames leaped up, the tension heightened, and except for the soft crackle from the big lumps of coal, the atmosphere seemed hushed as my mother's voice, clear and vivid, read on and on.

In those early school days it was from books that I gradually learned to appreciate great dramatic situations, tragedy, comedy, the thrill of travel and exploration, although as a very small girl this was mainly through my mother's reading aloud, and only later I entered the enchanted world for myself. And always, as the essential rule for life, and a source of beauty and spiritual comfort, I was taught to listen to the Bible. The rolling cadences of the psalms, the mournful echoes of the prophets, the triumph of Paul's proclamation of the Gospel, and the forceful simplicity

of the Gospels in the greatest story in the world, were my
daily food.

Books grew to become a large part of my world. Theatres
and cinemas were, of course, in the Puritan tradition,
entirely barred to me. The very smell of stuffiness and stale
cigarette smoke that was apparent when one passed their
open doors became a sign to me of dissolute living, for from
time to time my father held up to me the evils and immorality
of those who appeared upon the stage, and of the dramas
thereon enacted. He had a story he was fond of telling of a
devout lady who, taken to the theatre in the reign of Victoria,
bowed her head in prayer before the performance, and was
rebuked by her husband.

'You are not in church now, my dear', he whispered in
embarrassment and annoyance.

'Do you mean I must not pray in this building?', his gentle
wife asked. On being told it was unsuitable, she said: 'Very
well, I must leave this place at once!' and did so! This story
seemed an adequate (if extraordinary) reason to my father
for his stand in this matter, which was totally sincere; and he
was unable to see any possibility of another point of view
being reasonable. My mother never opposed him in this
matter.

But, although my father had this obstinate streak, this
inability to see another point of view, the apparent sternness
was often softened by his humour which would burst out
suddenly and unexpectedly, so that sitting at the dining-table
and recollecting an amusing event he would throw his head
back and laugh until the tears ran down his cheeks. Dabbing
helplessly at his eyes with his table napkin, he would be
unable to continue the meal. Every time the recollection
recurred, he was helpless again. The funny side of the story
had literally incapacitated him. It was impossible not to feel
drawn to a man who saw humour in small incidents, and

who often was seized with laughter so that at times his attitude to life was buoyant and even carefree.

Holidays in particular drew out the happy side of his nature, and my mother relaxed and shared his pleasure in freedom from duty.

I was about seven or eight years old when I was taken with them to Portishead, a little resort on the Bristol Channel where the air was bracing, and the rocky beach was an enchanted playground. Here we discovered a large boating lake. There were rowing boats and children's paddle-boats painted white and green. At first I was allowed a paddle-boat. The thrill of seeing the blunt nose pushing through the water, and the white froth spuming out from under the paddles was intoxicating; I chugged off to the far horizon and real adventure. The spring sunshine cast a pale golden light across the water; the stiff breeze caressed my cheeks, and whipped strands of hair across my eyes. My father took my mother out in a rowing boat. I watched him as he passed me, cloth cap back to front on his head, in his holiday mood when care was cast to the winds and he gave himself up to simple enjoyment. He was a man of the most innocent tastes and pleasures, unsophisticated and eager. My mother sitting opposite him was amused and delighted at his happiness; and their boat flashed past me where I was clanking away at the paddles. His oars were sweeping the water and dripping with myriads of dazzling golden drops as they lifted into the sunlight. Suddenly, flinging his head back he burst into loud song, which echoed across the empty sun-flecked lake: 'Here we row in our golden boat, golden boat, golden boat. . . .' The pale clear air resounded with the rising notes. Suddenly the great idea occurred.

'I can row too, I'm strong enough', I shouted across the water. My father paused in his singing, and looked at me meditatively.

'Very good exercise for the chest of course', he said, considering the thought.

In a few minutes I had discarded my first love, and was ensconced in a tiny rowing boat, having my first lesson in manipulating the oars, which were much heavier than they appeared, and my hands grew sore, and my arms ached. But if one is determined, nothing is impossible, and in half an hour I was rowing. Now the wind tugged wildly at my hair, and the air was full of the sound of the glittering water that danced, sparkled and lapped against the sides of the boat. It was a golden day.

My mother was happy when she sensed that my father was at peace. Her own true emotions seemed so hidden that she sometimes even seemed unaware of herself as a person. Each morning I watched her brushing carefully but disinterestedly the reddish fair hair, never bothering to change the style, always gazing at herself in the mirror with unseeing faraway eyes, her mind on other things.

Jigging up and down, examining her jewellery box, her brooches, and wreaking havoc in her drawer to her mild annoyance, I would urge her to use a little powder or make-up. Other mothers did. Why not mine? She rejected this utterly. 'I should look very silly', she said, and that was that. Nevertheless, she always looked fresh, and dressed well, often wearing soft shades of blue which matched her eyes.

It was, however, quite a surprise to me when an elderly admirer of hers stopped us one day in the fashionable Milsom Street. After bestowing various fulsome compliments upon her, which my mother received with courtesy but little interest, he turned to me.

'I wonder if you realise, my dear', he said, 'that your mother is a most handsome woman?'.

I was astonished. She looked quite ordinary to me, and was just my mother. I gazed at her with new awareness, and realised she was now blushing with some embarrassment. I felt that the old gentleman did not meet many nice ladies. Thus does familiarity breed contempt.

She had an amusing close friend, a Frenchwoman, who had been a colleague in the teaching world with her. I was devoted to 'Auntie France', who brought out in my mother a playful, humorous, more carefree side than I often observed. Witty, warm-hearted, not religious, this friend was very fond of my idealistic, sometimes unworldly mother. On one occasion, in my hearing, she took it upon herself to deliver a warning: 'One day, my little one', she said, addressing my mother affectionately, 'in your next reincarnation, mark my words, you will be totally bald. You have that beautiful hair and it means nothing to you. You do not bother with it, nor change the style, nor take any interest in it. You neglect yourself, thinking of that doctor of yours. You let your lovely figure go too. Yes! But of course that was your fault, Peganne.'

She turned to me with an admonishing look. It took me a long time to work out how I could be held responsible for this disaster!

Sometimes my mother showed a light-hearted gaiety of spirit. It was as if the solemnities and problems of life dropped from her for a while and her unquenchable spirit surged up in laughter. She had anxieties of many kinds, but from time to time they were wholly forgotten, and something of her natural happiness asserted itself. When the patients who came to consult my father each afternoon had departed, and the stifling quietness of the house during those hours was relaxed, she would sit at the piano and play some of the sentimental songs she had sung as a girl, not seriously but with a wealth of dramatic gesture, and the notes of 'Come into the garden, Maud' would echo out in the stately room, my mother assuming a false contralto; or else with a mock expression of solemnity she would sing 'I'd rather be an old man's darling than live and be a young man's slave!'. Coming into the room sometimes, my father would pause at the door, and stand there laughing, and the day would be bright and happy.

When she was out, spending long hours at committee meetings, I grew restless and uneasy, and walked round the great house, silent but for the maids downstairs in the kitchens, and I knew that life would be empty if she did not come back. Then panic seized me, and I could settle to nothing. Life was only complete if she was there. And so I was happy to follow her wherever she was prepared to take me, watching her in all she did, admiring the quick brain, the quiet confident manner, seeing the care she had for people in need or sorrow.

For it was no part of her belief that I should be sheltered from the unpleasant side of life. The poverty and sadness of others should be understood by me, and no age was too early to begin. It was because of this that I always seemed to be climbing after her: endless evil-smelling bare staircases in dingy houses in the poor part of the city. There would come her shy knock on a door, and some sick or aged person swathed in shawls would peer out of a damp room where washing seemed perpetually to hang, and would draw her in, clasping her hand. She made continuous unobtrusive journeys to certain families where she knew of great poverty or sickness, taking eggs regularly to a tubercular small boy, or some small practical gift to sick and elderly people, bringing something to comfort and help.

Much of the mutual happiness of my parents when they were together stemmed from their little plans to help alleviate need wherever it was found. Some of those she helped were poor women who came to her women's meeting on a Sunday afternoon, which she undertook with my father's sister, Mary.

It was strange to see two such totally different people working in harmony. My gentle rather ineffectual aunt in her old-fashioned clothes, quite out of touch with the everyday world, and my resolute mother pursuing her independent path, and retaining her clear outlook and understanding of the problems of the day, farseeing in making educational policies, wise in her counsel to the many who sought it, well-dressed, yet prepared to give herself to this work and to attempt to pass on something of her increasing faith. For this must, I think, be stressed. My mother had, I believe, a deep longing to find my father's assurance, inner serenity and peace in believing. She was aware that she was no spiritual athlete, as he was; she had an inner humility in matters of faith, and regarded herself as a failure in many ways. Yet I saw her Christian convictions grow in strength. She accepted stern disciplines and difficult routines which might have broken a weaker character, and she endured them quietly. Her faith, indeed, became different in kind.

She found in my father's home something she could not understand—conflicts over belief. Coming from a united happy family, where each member was accepted for themselves alone, she now faced a group who were united by basic love for each other, but torn apart over the things they most ardently held—their religious convictions. Perhaps it was not at first obvious that this was really a clash of character and temperament. My father who had a puritan simplicity, a clear-cut approach to right and wrong as he conceived it, could not be moved from a position he had taken up, if he believed it must, for conscience sake, be maintained. To him the Church was the body of believers in Christ. He could not agree with any form of worship other than the simple gathering at his meeting. In his eyes membership of the Church must be through an act of will alone, expressed in adult baptism which was undertaken after a conversion experience that alone could bring life-giving renewal of the spirit. Confirmation and infant baptism therefore were, on his conscience, unacceptable to him.

That my sisters could not agree with him was a grief to him. That they felt his views narrow and distasteful in face of the teaching of the Church during the centuries, was understandable but distressing to him. He had accepted their unhappiness within his meeting, drawing perhaps a little comfort from their emancipation and joy in the Church of England, and he never criticised their views. But he longed simply and ardently for their souls' salvation, and that they should experience the one thing he had found of reality and significance in life, his joy in believing in Christ as his personal Saviour. He and they could not, however, converse in these terms. They found his evangelical language embarrassing; he was hurt because they turned from him if he ever raised the one subject that mattered to him. He seemed to need no authoritarian support as they did in their Church. Completely independent of man, he looked to God alone, and from that great source drew an almost superhuman strength. But my sisters could not be blamed for being different. Indeed, in a way, we all were. When in need, we could draw on his strength, but we could not, as he did, stand entirely independent of others.

Perhaps it was strange that for a second time he had married an Anglican. He was much criticised by the Brethren for marrying someone of 'unsound' views. It is astonishing to remember his acceptance of their attitude. But in his heart he felt he had been 'led of the Lord', and he knew it might be misunderstood. How disastrous it is when men try and direct the sincere conscience of others. He needed a quick intelligence, a lively intellect to match his, and also, I think, one who was not afraid to broaden his views, for he wanted a wife he could respect. He saw that my mother was a sincere Christian, and no doubt hoped she would grow fully to understand his views. I do not know what was in his mind or hers; I know it distressed her that the greatest uniting force in the world, for she believed the Christian faith could be this, had caused these conflicts and misunderstandings in his family. Neither side, it appeared, could truly accept the validity of the other's vision. There was a battleground in the one place where there should have been peace and happiness, and she found she stood on the other side from her husband. What anguished questionings she endured I do not know. Nor what tensions arose when I was baptised privately, in secret almost, in our home. For it was a baptism of which my father could not have approved, but I believe my mother was adamant, and one of my sisters acted as my godmother.

Nor do I know how gently, how persuasively my father in his assured belief talked and reasoned with her. But over the months and years as husband and wife went often to a different place of worship, my mother could see no way out of the impasse. Moreover, in the Brethren meeting where she accompanied him from time to time, she saw a sincerity and commitment in many who worshipped there that gave her cause to think deeply, and to wonder whether it were possible that her husband, whom she admired, whose medical skill was outstanding, whose piety mingled with warmth, humour and kindness, might not be right. For here, among the Brethren, were people whose faith was very strong. But what of my sisters who had only found happiness and emancipation, and a life-giving breadth of vision in the Church of England? Why could they not all accept each other's different paths? Perhaps she reasoned so. She was at least prepared to listen to my father, and he to persuade. Referring her to the Scriptures, to the simple purity of worship in his meeting as it seemed to him, to its dependence on no state, no priest, but only on the Lord, he must have swayed her to a partial acceptance of his belief.

What sadness she experienced I do not know, but three years after her marriage my mother was baptised as an adult, and took the irrevocable step of joining her husband. She never spoke of that day except to say briefly once, 'It was an ordeal'. It was the moment, I grew to realise later, when she said farewell with clear sight and, I think, sorrow to her past life, to her own family who could not understand this action and were full of deep regret, to her desires, emotions, and everything she had been. My mother was no puritan at heart. She loved life. But all she did was accomplished in love, so that she might support her husband, and bring up her child in a home that was not divided.

Today when all these matters are not of importance to the majority of people, the intensity of feeling aroused by her act may seem extraordinary. It was an example on a small scale, however, of the battle for freedom of conscience in matters of belief. My mother walked unhappily between those who would influence her to their way of thinking. In the struggle I sometimes felt she gave up something of her own identity.

I think it was at about this time that one of my sisters ceased to return home except at very rare intervals. She began to lead an independent life in London where she worked. When she did return briefly, I noticed—even as a tiny child—the sudden flash of warmth, the fleeting look of deep concern with which she and my father looked at each other, and I felt it was she, not I, who should have been in that home, and I knew that life has cruelties more refined than any weapons of torture, but it was not myself for whom I was sorry.

My mother never revealed her own questionings at this time. She never looked back, and as I later discovered, she was lost from that time onwards to those who had loved her, both friends and family. She made a new life. I still do not know if it satisfied her.

She now entered my father's territory as a stranger, and to some extent she remained so, for she never completely identified herself with it, although she walked in it serenely enough, as it appeared to those outside.

She remained firm on one point. The Brethren were fond of asking about the soul, and about one's walk with the Lord. Their questions came naturally and spontaneously to them. But she shrank from such spiritual obtrusiveness. I believe she guarded me from it as far as she could, with one exception. She acknowledged my father's concern in this matter. She knew he felt it his own burden of responsibility to wrestle for our souls' welfare, to agonise over us until we were safely in the Kingdom.

Why could he not rest, I have asked myself, in this anxiety? Why did he not leave this burden, as he did every other, with Christ? My mother knew that all he did was undertaken in love, but at times his happiness was almost destroyed by the depth of his concern.

Perhaps she tried gently to make him realise that faith cannot be forced. For I came to realise that she knew well that I lived in a world of spiritual warning. Some of the less imaginative of the Brethren, like many others of strong evangelical belief, sometimes crushed the very seed they tried so earnestly to plant. Of course it is vital that the great Christian truths must be planted like seeds in the minds of children. You cannot deprive them of your most precious possession hoping vaguely that they will one day, accidentally and with no help, discover it. But a seed with the tiny spark of life enclosed in it needs tending in an atmosphere of calm and care for its slow and hidden growth. If it is perpetually dug up and examined, it will surely die.

Thus my mother walked on the knife-edge of a dilemma:

how to support my father, yet see I was not subjected to pressures too severe. Gradually, I think, he relaxed, and as I grew older, he showed a gentleness and constraint that were in no small measure due to her. He, on his part, gently and irrevocably drew her into a small community who were united by bonds of love so strong that they are rarely seen in most churches and Christian groups, protective, caring, unyielding. She now began to live among people for whom every detail of life was 'laid before the Lord' with a simple sincerity that is difficult to describe. The concentration of their love for their Master could only be comprehended by those who have experienced it. Completely unquestioning, they faced the sorrows and joys of life as from the hand of God, and if men regarded them with scorn, incredulity, or more frequently with a total lack of interest, they gladly accepted it as their privilege to be considered fools for Christ's sake.

AUNT ANNIE

7

THE AUNTS

I SEEMED to have been born into a world of middle-aged aunts. Always dressed in black or grey, I never knew why— possibly they were in constant mourning for one or another of their vast clan—they seemed entirely to lack the youthful gaiety and modernity of other people's aunts. But they were certainly unusual.

Four of the aunts lived near us in Bath during my childhood, and made part of the strange pattern of an enclosed adult world in which I grew up. I think they must have finally pitched their tent to be near my father, as the last stage, or so they imagined, in their life's journey. For here they intended to settle, and finally to die, believing that he would sustain them. They were the products of a patriarchal society, and he was now the father-figure in their lives, one who in their eyes could do no wrong. They took no part in the normal social life of their day, but were given to various good works, chiefly religious in nature. The flood waters of the first quarter of the twentieth century seemed to have passed over them, leaving them like flotsam on some unfamiliar shore, from which they gazed wistfully back to a distant place and time where they had belonged, and to the powerful Victorian home whose piety had so firmly moulded them, so that it seemed they were unwilling—or unable—to adjust to the changing social pattern after the first world war, a pattern which they regarded with suspicion and some dismay.

I suspect, however, that their devotion to my father may have been much strained when he married again, and I feel it must have been a profound shock to them. In varying degrees they had supported or assisted in his ménage during the years after his first wife died, and had helped their sister Edith when it was necessary. With his remarriage, they became in effect camp followers, a little outside the inner circle of his household. The foundation of their life was shaken. For my father had brought into the family a woman who was modern in outlook for her time, emancipated in her academic achievements, and prominent in the educational world; she dressed well and had an apparent poise, and a calm control of any situation that arose. At first, I am sure, they could see none of the uncertainties in her mind, nor the loneliness and inner fearfulness which had created in her the desire to turn to one whom she could love and respect. There was a barrier between them and her. My mother was not of their kind.

Divergent in character as they all were, they shared one single aim which united them. It was the pursuit of goodness as they understood it, based on Biblical precepts. They have long been dead now, but I recall them as if it was but yesterday, and I can hear in imagination their quick conversation.

Aunt Annie bustled. She was one of the most emancipated of the aunts. She was short, had silky soft brown hair in a tiny bun, and twinkling observant dark eyes. She was always in a hurry, attended many committees connected with nursing, and helped with various meetings in the parish church nearby. For Aunt Annie had left the Brethren in those days at St Bartholomew's Hospital. She showed a sturdy independence of spirit that in no way conflicted with her love for her quiet puritan sisters whom she cared for busily and devotedly.

She and Aunt Jennie and later Aunt Edith, when ill health

forced her to give up the training of missionaries in London, all spinsters, lived in a tiny attic flat at the top of a tall Georgian house whose blackened stone had long since lost its pristine beauty, so that it appeared rather forbidding from outside. From their windows, however, the Aunts gazed down over the city of Bath, and away to the hills beyond, a panoramic view about which they gently expatiated, indicating that the flat might be awkward, but it was, however, exceedingly inexpensive and all was compensated for by the vista outside. For the aunts never grumbled, never lamented that their income was tiny and dwindling, that they were often hard put to it to keep body and soul together. Their dark neat dresses, some twenty years out of fashion, were turned, reshaped, and occasionally shortened a trifle by a pale little dressmaker nearby, who understood their needs. They were quietly happy in that they accepted without a murmur all that life sent them, for they came of one of the most disciplined groups English society has produced. There was a stoical attitude to hardship. Money was a taboo subject. If the heart was at peace with God, then one had unlimited wealth of the spirit, and what more could one ask for?

Aunt Mary, a widow, the passionate sister, lived near them in a gloomier ground floor flat alone, as befitted her married status. I suspect also that, having given all her love to her husband, she could not face living within the close family group again. She was essentially kind, but apt to be intense. Yet she depended on the others, none the less.

Aunt Annie, then, trotting from flat to flat, hurrying round to consult my father about one matter or another, was the lively active sister. She had a special concern for Jennet, whose health was 'delicate', for she had had serious 'operations'; I could never, to my regret, discover any details—they were unmentionable. On her visits to us, Aunt Annie invariably appeared to be in a hurry. A loud rat-tat on the brass door knocker, a prolonged ring, and she would hasten briskly in, eager to tell us tit-bits of news, to enlist my father's advice. Aunt Jen's sciatica was very bad today; Mr Brewster in the bottom flat in their house must be burning incense again, the smell was intolerable; what could be done? There was to be a sale of work in the hall of the parish church. Would my mother be going?

I liked Aunt Annie. She had vitality, and could play vigorous games of make-believe when, from time to time, she came to look after me when my mother was ill and I had some childish ailment. She was a superb nurse. On these occasions she would arrive in the nursery beaming and twinkling. Out of a rather ancient black capacious bag she would produce a spotless white overall, which she donned with evident pleasure. It smelt of clean kitchen soap and starch and was always freshly laundered. No one could wash fevered brows better than Aunt Annie, whose gentle firm hands had a soothing quality, and the while she would tell tales of her family and the multifarious sicknesses at which she had attended, and the journeys she had made to visit her many relatives. Aunt Eliza, Uncle Mills, Uncle Everard, Aunt Emma, Cousin James, Cousin Lettice, the relatives passed before me in an endless stream, and I pictured them ceaselessly journeying from one end of the country to the other to visit each other. My father's was indeed a vast and varied family, all inexplicably eager to meet each other at regular intervals.

It was with Aunt Annie that I travelled in imagination through St Bartholomew's Hospital, during the latter years of the reign of Queen Victoria. I saw those scrubbed bare boards, smelt the strong carbolic odour that pervaded the air, gazed on the white beds in the barrack-like long wards. I was curious and interested in any crumbs of medical

knowledge I could gather up, and often prevailed on Aunt
Annie to discuss horrific diseases and medical treatments. We
had lurid conversations. I questioned her about matters my
father would never discuss. Sinister words dropped from the
lips of the many missionaries who constantly came to our
house, lunched with us, and were treated free of charge by
my father.

'Aunt Annie, what is bubonic plague? How do rats bring
it?'

'What do you feel like when you are getting cholera?'

'Have you nursed yellow fever?'

Together we would nod our heads in the firelight over the
ailments of mankind.

'What does it feel like to have a baby, Aunt Annie?'

As my aunt was a spinster, it is surprising that I regarded
her as a mine of information on a subject about which my
parents were peculiarly reticent, but it was necessary to
discover the truth. All in all I learned a lot from my maiden
aunt; I think we shared a somewhat earthy interest in
biological matters. Moreover I felt relaxed with her for she
did not fall into spiritual discourse with no warning as the
other aunts were apt to do. I suppose she was an activist,
while they had more of the contemplative streak in their
character, while my father in some remarkable way combined
the two. My aunt was careful to show my sisters especial
affection, and this was just. Being more practical and down
to earth than my father in assessing their needs, she understood their longing for a form of worship which satisfied their
full nature. She especially asserted her Anglicanism for them,
not to oppose her brother so much as to support two girls
who could not make their father understand that the manner
of his religious observance in the Plymouth Brethren starved
the sensuous side of their natures, and denied their need to
find God in a way that was natural to them. My aunt

attempted sturdily to bridge the gap between them. She loved her brother but was not in awe of him, and was more clear-sighted in some ways than her sisters. I think at times she could be fiery, but this was kept under stern control, and if she ever flared up it was in defence of someone rather than as an attack.

Aunt Jennie was a different type of character in every way. It was quite an undertaking to pay her the regular visit to enquire after her health. On opening the heavy door from the street in Portland Place, you faced the door of the ground floor flat, whereupon your nostrils were assailed by such an appalling odour of incense and poodle combined, why we never knew—it was a surprising mixture—that you were nearly knocked backwards. Whether Mr Brewster burnt incense as a follower of some Eastern religion, or whether he did it to mask the smell of his ageing dog, it was impossible to tell. It was even more embarrassing to encounter him in the hall. Wearing a grey overcoat with a nipped-in waist that was clearly supposed to be elegant, with the largest Persian lamb fur collar on it that I have ever seen, he minced out in his pointed black shoes. Were it not for Mr Brewster, the full meaning of the word 'minced' might have eluded me. But once having seen him, it became clear. His feet turned outwards; he walked delicately and disdainfully like an aged dancer, his dog on a leash beside him walking a little in the same manner. His pallid countenance—his was a thin and pointed face—surmounted by a slender homburg hat exactly straight on his head, showed no reaction when one said 'Good morning'. There was the faintest inclination of the hat, and a blank and haughty stare—perhaps hardly robust enough to be called a stare—it was a bare recognition; and he passed on, ignoring one's presence, while his 'man', peering out of the door of his flat to see him go, leered a little as we mounted the stairs to ascend to the top flat to see my aunt.

Having rung the first bell at street level, the chances were that my aunt would be awaiting our arrival, as somewhat breathless we climbed higher and higher to her door. We would gaze up at the last flight, and there she used to stand, peering down at us over the banisters, her nose wrinkled up, and pinched between her fingers, indicating her displeasure at the smell from below. Then her rather droll face would crease into a smile.

'So you have come to commiserate with your aged aunt! Come in, my dearest child.'

Envisaging some major calamity that must have befallen her, I would answer:

'What has happened to you, Aunt Jenny? Is anything the matter?' I was always hopeful that the secret details of the operations on Aunt J. would be revealed. But no.

'My dear child, I am *afflicted*.'

I waited breathless.

'It is that terrible corn again. My toe is causing me excruciating pain. You see I am wearing these old slippers.' I gazed at her feet in disappointment. Aunt Jennie then would lead us up the stairs, clasping one hip which was 'full of rheumatism'.

She was a lovable character. Good-tempered, thinking little of herself, she always looked up to the other members of her family, believing them much more gifted than she was. Somehow, she seemed to have passed her life drifting into whatever was convenient to others, looking after a cousin's children here, caring for elderly relatives there. She was rueful, unselfish, was unfailingly defeated in argument by her sometimes overpowering sisters, and had the kindest of hearts. Like all the family, she lived with vivid memories of her parents to whom she had been entirely devoted. Because of this, perhaps, she had remained in the Brethren meeting, helping with sundry good works in an unostentatious way, mothers' meetings, a Bible class for women, and she seemed to lead a life remote from the bustle of the world. I grew to feel that, in a way, she had never quite grown up. Her bedroom was full of photographs of astonishing numbers of relatives, their cousins, aunts, uncles and children. She seemed to linger on as a wistful spectator of past happiness, when all the children were young, and she was a tomboyish girl, happy and carefree, and always at hand to 'help mother' with the younger children.

Her Christian faith, too, seemed to be a quiet routine inherited from her childhood. It consisted of regular and constant reading of her large black Bible, in which she had carefully underlined many verses of help and consolation with ruler and ink, and attendance at the meeting of the Plymouth Brethren each Sunday morning; it was a long walk for her, but she had to be really ill to miss it. She sat there, eyes shut, asleep perhaps I thought, but I believe she was really carried away in thought to past days when she had been happy, sitting in another meeting long ago beside Papa and Mama whom she had loved so much, and who had clearly been so much more powerful and exciting than she could ever hope to be. Any criticism of the Brethren by my sisters distressed her, for I think any conflict was unspeakably painful to her. She did not seem to question authority, nor to make demands on other people, but wanted to be left in her small world where she worshipped God in simplicity of heart, for she had no guile, no malice, only a total lack of understanding of life outside her limited sphere.

Aunt Mary, the widow, was the saddest of the aunts, as I remember her. In her rather gloomy flat she grieved in solitude for the husband to whom she had been devoted, and she became something of a recluse except for her Sunday pilgrimage to the meeting, and to a Women's Bible Class which was held each Sunday afternoon in a rather poor part of the city. This was the one activity that seemed to revive her vitality. With the women who were fond of her because of her rather emotional sympathy and kindness for them, she responded, showing an affectionate concern for them. She was devoted to my mother, who helped her with this work at one time, and who, sensitive herself, showed her the sympathy for which she craved; and in our house the latent sense of humour would occasionally show itself. We would tell her some funny story, and she would laugh until the tears ran down her pale sad face, and then she would take me in her arms in a gesture that emphasised the emptiness of her life, exclaiming, 'My beloved child, what should I do without you?'.

She was deeply, soberly devout, but the Brethren meeting had the unfailing effect of causing her to fall into heavy sleep. Sunday by Sunday, she bowed in prayer, and without fail a gentle snoring would soon be heard. My mother and father, on the seat in front of her, would turn round and try to rouse her, but to no avail. Aunt Mary slept on, oblivious of the ministry of 'the Saints'.

She was at heart a gentle, sweet-natured woman, lonely, and sad. Sometimes she used to come quietly into the nursery and sit by my bed in the evening. It was part of the essential routine in Plymouth Brethren households that the Bible was read morning and evening, to the young children as well as the older members of the family. There is a certain granite strength in people of 'The Book', to whatever sect or denomination they belong. Something of the spirit of the prophets and early Christians enters into the soul; you cannot be touched by the Word of God and remain impervious to it. It is common now to reject it utterly. But those who still find in it their inspiration become changed people—imperceptibly, but steadily.

Thus Aunt Mary played her part in trying to bring one

small girl into the fold. It was a gentle part like the brushing of the wings of a moth against the cheek, but the tiny sensation remained, fluttering, imprisoned in the memory; and once again I hear the quiet voice reading one of the psalms to me before the light is turned out, and I feel again the peace of that quiet room where evening by evening I was committed to the Lord:

'I sought the Lord, and he heard me, and delivered me from all my fears. They looked unto him and were lightened: and their faces were not ashamed. This poor man cried, and the Lord heard him, and saved him out of all his troubles.'

And I, drowsily listening, was enfolded by quietness and peace.

What love affairs the unmarried aunts may have experienced, if any, I never knew. To me, as I look back, they appear almost sexless in their dark dresses, with the inevitable 'modesty vest' at the neck, in the fashion of their day. Aunt Jenny once appeared on the verge of revealing some thwarted love affair for a distant cousin. The story never unwound, however. Her temerity in beginning it overcame her, and the door to the past which had begun so tantalisingly to open, was quickly shut before one could see within.

They were so unlike my mother in every way that in my childish mind 'the aunts' became a collective term symbolic of an alien background to life, that part which was drawn in sombre muted colours. I wanted the foreground to be painted in brilliant vivid splashes of light, I wanted it to be full of contrast, gaiety and movement. As a child I was barely conscious of this, but I grew to feel the life of my father's sisters seemed so circumscribed, so inward-looking, that I found it saddening. I did not fit into their picture, for instinctively, although I could not express this, I felt my mother and I saw

life with different eyes. Yet it was they who struggled to ease
my path when it seemed I might be left alone for ever in their
world. I was to be without my mother for three months and
to know that she might never come back, and the word death
became a menacing and real terror to me during my first
year at school. At this time I was six years old.

There was a light beside my mother's bed, I remember,
when I went in to say goodnight that evening. She looked
flushed and not herself, but she was not robust at that time,
and I did not sense anything unusual, until she held out her
hand and said with an unusually brilliant smile,

'Such a nuisance. I am to have an operation tomorrow.
It's only my appendix.'

My wandering thoughts focused, the moment became hard
and glaring.

'Where are you going?'

She would be only a street or two away, in a nursing home
she told me; it was quite near, and we should see each other.
But a cold desolation crept over me. My mother was my
life, my *alter ego*. She softened the hardness, laughed at
difficult situations, interpreted my sometimes inexplicable
father, eased my path, and found a host of tiny pleasures we
could both enjoy, almost in secret. Now I was to be left alone
and nothing could compensate for her departure. I seized
her hand, begged her not to stay away long, asked if she was
in pain, and then as I saw the tears in her eyes, began to
weep, until my father coming in and finding us, gently took
me to my own room and said I must not upset my mother.
He looked withdrawn, anxious. I was alone.

The next day my mother was taken away by car, and
Aunt Annie moved into our home, full of zeal and energy
and promises of many games we would play together. But
this time it seemed a hollow mockery. I wanted no one. Aunt
Jennie and Aunt Mary arrived at frequent intervals, and

conferred in low voices. As the days passed, they and the maids seemed to fall silent when I approached, gazing at me with a sort of apprehension and pity. My father prayed for my mother's recovery at family prayers, committing her to the will of God, and there was a white anguished look about him. What childish terrors now gripped me I do not remember. It appears I heard the maids saying to each other that I should never see my mother again. I did not know that she had developed a most serious complication, and my father was faced with the prospect of losing his second wife. All I knew was that life was barren and meaningless, and I belonged nowhere and cared for no one, for I was forbidden to see my mother in spite of passionate daily requests.

I do remember that after an eternity of lost time, when at last I was allowed to visit her, and I saw her sitting propped up in bed, as if she was shrinking into a sea of whiteness, I fell into her arms in a torrent of weeping, laying my head beside hers on the high bank of snowy pillows. She and I were together again in a close relationship that the aunts could never share, for it was we, not they who were outsiders in a land where we did not really belong.

Weeks later when my mother was still not able to walk, she was taken out in a bath-chair drawn by an aged man through the Victoria Park. Many of these invalid carriages were to be seen in those days and were often used for the sick people who came to Bath to take the waters. They were like giant push-chairs with heavy black hoods and glass windows in the front. The invalid was hermetically sealed inside, and covered with rugs in the body of the chair. The window would be lowered only if the weather was favourable and the invalid was then able to take the air. To this day I cannot look at the few remaining bath-chairs that are now exhibited as curiosities without a shudder and a feeling of gloom. I walkde gravely beside my mother's chair each afternoon; and as her grip on life grew stronger my spirit at last soared up again, and the flowers seemed more brightly coloured, and the foliage of the great trees beneath which we passed sheltered us benignly once more, for the menacing clouds had rolled away at last.

The aunts played a decreasing part in my life as the years went by. In some fashion I felt they missed much of the on-going movement of life. I was intolerant of their quiet lives, although I could recognise their total integrity, their desire to do nothing but was right or in line with God's will.

I think now that they were proud and independent people who would have died rather than ask for help, or discuss difficulties. They lived with spartan simplicity, eating the plainest meals, having no holidays, never dreaming of buying new possessions. Each Christmas and birthday, from the earliest days I can recollect, each aunt presented me with half a crown, carefully wrapped up in white paper. It was wealth to me, but I did not then realise it was also wealth to them. I have no doubt, however, that my father helped them in many ways, and in return they watched his every move with concentrated devotion.

The pattern of their lives seemed to fall into place only if linked with his. Without him their days lacked a central pivotal point. He was the centre of a circle. They moved to and fro on the circumference, and outside of it, I think their life would have lacked validity or purpose. His faith was their faith. Christ was more real to them all than those who lived beside them, for they walked as strangers and pilgrims who sought a heavenly city. Nothing else mattered.

There was a strange unworldliness about my middle-aged aunts. Their undeviating pursuit of goodness stemmed from purity of heart and sincerity of intention planted and fostered in their lives from birth by their idealistic God-fearing parents. Goodness meant little to them apart from a personal faith in Christ, which was the motive force of their activities and had driven two of them to pioneer as missionaries in conditions of great hardship in inland China. But for most of them their faith was, I believe, a garrison for their hearts, a support for their frailties and a comfort in the storms of life; it was not a divine discontent of spirit driving them to move out of their enclosed spiritual society into the world of their day to seek friendship and understanding with the sinner and the misfit. Personal piety made them a little apart. For, although all were glad to draw others *into* their Christian circle to share their faith, I think they found it difficult to leave it except with missionary intention, and in this they were not unlike many staunch evangelicals of their time and sometimes of today.

UNCLE GEORGE

8

UNCLE GEORGE

As I turn this page, I pause and look closely. I am stabbed a little, I think, by this memory. There you are, Uncle George, smiling at me in that whimsical, almost provocative way as you did when I first saw you. It was, I suppose, early in the nineteen-twenties, for I was seven years old, I think, and, apart from my parents, you have remained more vivid in my mind than any other relative. How odd that this should be so, because I think I only saw you four times in my life. But you seemed to belong to a different world, and in our home you were an outsider. This was not because you were unwelcome, but because you did not fit into the required pattern, and you knew it. For one thing it was hinted at, although hardly ever mentioned, that you had lost your faith.

Your whole way of life was new to me. You were a chain smoker and that was hardly acceptable in our house. I loved the smell that lingered about you. It was worldly, I thought. You only rarely came to family prayers and you looked stiff and uncomfortable when you did, and my mother looked concerned and distressed for you. I am certain she wished you could have the joy of my father's unswerving faith, but life had taken all hope of that from you somewhere in the dark years of the first world war.

You looked different, too, in some way. Your dark blue London suits gave you the air of a man of the world, and your

119

tanned face indicated that you were a traveller, and had lived abroad. But whatever you did, your irrepressible humour broke out again and again although in a way this often hid the personality buried beneath it.

As I look back across the dividing years, it is your eyes I remember most vividly, smiling, for we often laughed together, but sometimes questioning, guarded; and the feel of your firm protecting hand as we walked through those Devonshire lanes together. I would have followed you anywhere. 'Don't forget your old uncle,' you said, looking down at me when you went away, and you bent down and kissed me a little shyly, and there was a sadness in your face. You never came back to us. So I must look back and piece together those fragmented memories, so few, but so significant, and try and remember all I was told about you.

Uncle George was the second child and only son of my grandfather, the London vicar. He was my mother's only brother, not quite two years younger than she, and her accounts of his escapades were among my favourite stories in childhood. Always in trouble, often attempting some daring feat that scared his family almost past bearing, he seemed to bring frequent laughter into their lives. My mother smiled over those recollections of his surging high spirits, and all the ploys he concocted with her. It was clear that those memories were for her a sequence of sunlit laughter-filled days that were full of happiness. It was transparently clear that this gay and reckless boy was the centre of her life.

All three children loved their vicar father—that compassionate broad-minded man who was concerned to give his children the best in education, literature and drama, and to let them savour all the excitements and interests of late Victorian London. The little diary he kept when the children were small, brief as are its entries, vividly suggest happy days packed full of movement and interest:

'Long rides with little brother in handcarriage to Kensington', states one, written for my mother when she was a tiny child.

'Broadstairs. Digging, paddling, goat-chaise', runs another entry describing a summer holiday.

'The Queen's Jubilee. Saw the preparations in Kensington and Piccadilly decorated with flags', is written in 1887.

One can picture the Vicar in frock coat and flat-topped clerical hat on his reddish hair, a sturdy rather squarely-built man, leading his two small eager children, one on either side, as they walked entranced along the gaily decorated streets. London was 'en fête'. My mother remembered all her life seeing the old Queen. 'She was the tiniest lady I had ever seen', she said in later years. 'She seemed dwarfed by all the pomp and ceremonial.'

When my mother and her brother were in their teens, the father records that they and their little sister went to the 'Bishop of London's garden party' and 'Olympia' and later that they 'visited the Royal Wedding gifts'—of the Prince of Wales and Princess Alexandra. Each day was to be packed with interest and happy activity.

In all the stories my mother recounted her brother George was the epitome of the gaiety for which I believe she and I both longed. My mother sometimes revealed a hidden desire to shock pompous or affected people, and it pleased her that her earliest memory of my uncle was when he slipped out of the house one morning at the age of three, removed the tiresome restricting clothing such as small boys wore in the last quarter of Victoria's reign, and proceeded to dance with happy abandon stark naked on the lawn in the front garden to the amusement of the passers-by, until a particularly prudish lady, shocked at the uninhibited child, hastily rang the front door bell to report the incident. My grandmother, who always seems to have been sensitive to the disapproval of powerful parishioners—she was tiny in stature, gentle, and a little inclined to be anxious—hastened out to scoop up the offender under her arm and remove him from the public gaze.

When he was a little older, he used to watch the building of a tall new house near the vicarage, and one day he again vanished from home. Soon, agitated passers-by rang the front door bell. George had somehow ascended the scaffolding like a monkey, and having triumphantly reached the skeleton roof-top, was sitting on a cross-beam over a yawning drop to the ground many feet below. A large crowd gathered to watch him—it would not be the only time in his life—the police arrived, and my grandmother rushed out to the scene, and looked up shocked and greatly alarmed. One false step, and clearly he would be killed. But it was she who, keeping her head, talked to him with a supreme effort in tones of icy authority, and heart in mouth watched him slowly inch his way down to the ground and safety, triumphant at his achievement.

When he grew older, he was sent to St Paul's School, where he laughed and joked his way through life, barely bothering to develop his astonishing flair for the classics whereby he composed poetry in Greek or Latin as easily as in English. At the end of the day he would burst into the house, flinging his satchel into the air, leaping over the back of the sofa, and often he would sing the popular songs of the day with a wealth of drama and verve, only sobering down from time to time to settle to work.

The sudden tragic death of my grandfather from a haemorrhage eventually brought harsh reality into his days, and changed the course of his life, which had been geared towards an Oxford scholarship. Now there was no money, and a post in the Admiralty was found and George started to work instead of play; but he had to begin at the bottom of the ladder.

There was no doubt that the vicarage children had had a happy childhood. It was, therefore, the more inexplicable that my mother and uncle eventually drifted apart so finally and irrevocably.

I did not know when I first saw him that he was already a sick man. My mother then explained to me gravely that he was worn out by a position of great responsibility in the first world war, in which the lives of many men depended on him. My uncle had refused all leave, never once coming home from the Mediterranean during the entire war, and in consequence of this his health had broken down, and he had now to rest and recuperate for a long time. The war had wrecked his life in more than one way. Because of the importance of his work, the Admiralty had refused to allow him to join one of the Services, and bitterly he had seen many of his friends killed. I still have his medals awarded by other countries for his work, which commemorated honours and distinctions he never mentioned. They did not compensate for the loss of friends and faith. As I look back, I believe that religiosity was no good to a man who had loved his fellow men, and now felt he was alone, with little to live for. He was too honest to deny that he now did not know where he stood in matters of belief. His humour never deserted him, however, nor his kindly tolerance of people. I think my mother's marriage to the puritan doctor had saddened him. The laughter they had shared was somehow extinguished. It was as if he and my father could not find any common meeting ground, and could only view each other with kindliness but with a total lack of comprehension of the other's outlook, and my mother walked uneasily between them.

In a South Devonshire fishing village where we were

staying on holiday one summer he first came to us, and the holiday became a golden stretch of days for me. When the dark-haired man came shyly into the little sitting-room of our holiday lodgings, bringing a feeling of suppressed vitality and, even then, leashed energy with him, I sensed—I know not how—that he would only belong to us for a short time, for he was not of our world, and I must make the most of the days given us. For me, it was a sort of love at first sight.

He sat a little stiffly on the chair opposite me at the lunch table which was covered with a white linen cloth, and which seemed so small compared with the large dignified table at home. My father began the meal as usual by 'giving thanks' for it. As he said the grace, I deliberately kept my eyes wide open to see whether Uncle George closed his. He did not. We gazed at each other questioningly, then his face creased into a sudden conspiratorial smile, and he deliberately winked. Delighted, I attempted to wink back, and he immediately put on a very pious and holy expression, looking at me with mock reproof. After this I was his for life, and it was a measure of his kindness that he endured my demands so patiently.

Each morning I led him to my favourite places. We sat pensively on the hulls of upturned fishing boats, and Uncle George looked out at the foaming waves that crashed on the large, smooth white pebbles so that there was a continuous grinding sound as the sea sucked them back a little, then hurled them forward, creating great stone shelves along the beach in new formations each day. Above us the gulls swooped and dived over the bits of rotting fish that lay near the boats, and their restless cry awoke an answering echo in his thoughts, I believe, for he gazed away into the distance almost longingly, blowing smoke rings from time to time, and sometimes talking about his journeys to the East.

We sometimes wandered up the cliff path with its precipitous drop edged by the yellow gorse bushes, alive with the humming of bees, and in the grass at our feet the grasshoppers clicked and stirred constantly. The red cliffs crumbled away a little more each year and sometimes we lay on the grass peering over the deep gashes caused by falls of rock which lay in jumbled masses far below.

At first there was one place to which I did not take him. I had discovered one day the cemetery in the fields behind our lodgings. I used to slip out alone before breakfast, when the dew was thick on the grass, and the early sun was glistening on the dazzling drops of moisture, to wander down the road, and to steal through the iron gates of this burial ground. I had no one to play with, and here I discovered there were very delectable little statues, which for some unknown reason filled my imaginative soul with much joy. Many plump little naked cherubs were festooned in various attitudes on the stone memorials, some leaping upwards, pointing to the sky. Others stood with meek and downcast gaze, wings neatly folded, hands demurely clasped together in an attitude of prayer. I used to go from one to the other and stroke them and examine the seraphic expressions of those who looked heavenwards. I am unable to account for this peculiar and morbid predilection. I think I wove stories around them. They seemed to be waiting there each day for me to come and play with them. But it was a private closely guarded pleasure, so I told no one where I went. The only person who ever saw me at that early hour was the old wrinkled brown-faced 'mackerel man' carrying home the early catch in a large basket. He chatted to me in the broad Devon dialect and always let me look at the blue lobsters and crabs with their waving claws.

I suppose I was lost one morning, and Uncle George came to look for me. Sitting on a grave, lost in meditation with one arm around a little cherub, I was discovered by my uncle. He looked at me questioningly for a long moment, some unexpressed emotion hidden in his dark eyes. Then he calmly sat down on the white marble memorial beside me and lit a cigarette.

'Margaret Anne,' he said—he always called me by both names—'why do you come here?'.

I looked awkwardly down at my feet, pushed a pebble across the path under my shoe, then looked up a little furtively to see if he was laughing at me. But his face was grave and still. Presently, as if he had all the time in the world to spare, he meditatively blew a few perfect smoke rings. I followed their formation and disappearance in the sunshine, and was aware of the light wisps of cloud—a mackerel sky —which promised a day of great heat. Uncle George was still waiting for an answer, and I saw he was prepared to sit there indefinitely.

'Well, I love these little angels. I play with them. They've got names', I said rather lamely and anxiously. I could not bear that he should laugh at me. But my uncle was entirely solemn for once, looking at me with a strange deep look which even now I remember. So I hastily added, '*Please* don't tell anyone about them, but you can come here if you like, because I come before breakfast every morning. There's a lot of them and I'll show you the nicest ones.'

His eyes were smiling again as I led him from one grave to another pointing out my favourite statuary. Then he took my hand gently, and said,

'We'll not say a word. Come now, or we'll *both* be in trouble.'

Every morning after that Uncle George visited the cemetery with me and had a smoke, while I visited my cherubs. Then quickly we slipped into the house together and sat on the little chintz-covered chairs in the tiny sitting-room for family prayers before breakfast.

Not much later he went away, and he never stayed with us again. I do not know why this was. I do not even remember any suggestion that he should come back. Knowing that he was in my father's eyes an 'unbeliever', did he feel awkward and out of place in our home? 'Poor George', my father said briefly when he was mentioned, and the subject was closed.

Occasionally he wrote a tiny scrawled letter to my mother in an almost illegible careless hand:

'Dear old girl,
How goes it? Keep your pecker up. Hope to see you sometime.

Your loving brother,
George.'

As I look back, I believe there was much pathos in these letters. He and my mother had been very close to each other, but he must have felt he no longer fitted into the life she had deliberately chosen for herself, and for her sake he may have been unwilling to disturb its equilibrium. I believe that my mother, over-sensitive to the rather sober and solemn atmosphere of the house which she had inherited, did not encourage him to come, feeling that he was not at ease in her home. Sometimes she looked sad when the little letters came, but she never revealed the cause.

Two or three times only she took me away to visit him in after years. The meeting was happy and he was clearly delighted to see us again. But it was sad to see him growing older, greyer, uncaring about himself, not fit now to work, and spending his time smoking and reading. Books were piled all around him, on table and floor in his lodgings; the majority were copies of the classics from which he knew unlimited passages by heart. Once he picked up a copy of Vergil and read it aloud to us, dramatically declaiming the rolling emphatic Latin periods. On the second visit he said, 'Here's something for you. I bought it for sixpence on a junk stall. You'll never get one like this!'

He searched among piles of books in the corner and at last unearthed a tiny shabby-looking little volume with a stained vellum cover. It was a 1642 Elzevir edition of Virgil's Aeneid. Elzevir was the name of a family of late sixteenth and seventeenth century Dutch printers, whose noted editions of the classics are much valued by collectors. It was one of his greatest treasures, and it was typical that he should almost carelessly give it away.

His wit never died. I said to him on one of our visits,

'Can you make up poetry about *anything*, Uncle George?'

'Try me, Margaret Anne', he said, the dark eyes lighting up with a trace of their old brilliance.

'Well now . . . you couldn't do one on "A Parish Magazine" I'm sure', I said. I am quite unable to understand why, from my background, this odd subject floated into my mind. Perhaps I could not fit him into my conception of a vicar's son, and my idea of vicars was inextricably bound up with earnest ladies distributing magazines. Whatever the thought that prompted it, this challenge did not deter my uncle. He flung his head back, laughed, and started almost immediately, and a humorous poem poured out of him, gently mocking, perfect in rhythm and cadence.

Whenever he looked at my mother, my uncle's eyes were gentle, even, I think pitying, although it was difficult to analyse that expression. She, I think, looked at him almost in despair, across an ever-widening gulf. She had become over the years a deeply religious woman, straining to keep up with and share my father's thoughts and aspirations. I believe her brother knew that her way was sometimes lonely and hard. Eventually each withdrew more and more into their own private world, and communication between them seemed to perish. Sometimes Uncle George wrote to me also in his illegible scrawling hand:

'Dear Margaret Anne,
    How are you? Don't forget your poor old uncle. Are you being good at school? Not too good, I hope! Have a lot of fun.
                                        Your loving Uncle.'

Somewhere in all this I grew conscious of witnessing a tragedy: that of a lonely affectionate man who, with little but his humour and his innately stoical nature to sustain him, lost his health and his happiness. This may, in part, have been due to his inability to understand my father who perhaps seemed to him to exert, even if unconsciously, too powerful an influence over my mother, for he had in some subtle way altered her, and moulded her to a pattern which to my uncle was an alien one. In the end I believe my uncle turned away quite deliberately from our life, partly for his sister's sake. He never married. Sought after by many girls as a young man, he was not accepted by the only one he wanted. That was the end for him. He was not interested in the second best.

I ask myself as I look closely at the eager lively man in the photograph, whom I remember so well, what did the Christian faith as expressed in my home do to him? Was it too exclusive, too inward-looking, manifesting itself strongly in certain rules and precepts, so that there was not room for a warm-hearted man who did not conform to its patterns? It should surely have brought comfort and solace to one who was lonely and ill, and who needed to be accepted just as he was. Insofar as it did not, it is a measure of our failure. I too am not exempt from blame, for I had left childhood when eventually he died alone, and I failed to understand his need. Surgery could not cure the advanced cancer caused by excessive smoking.

An untidy brown paper parcel arrived for me by post shortly before this. It was unexpected, and I was surprised to see the unmistakable scrawled writing on the rather torn paper. Inside, wrapped in cotton wool, was a silver vase, one of his few treasures. A tiny note lay in it:

'For your birthday.
   I hope it will hold some roses for you.'

I knew it was his farewell.

MY FATHER AND ONE OF HIS ROOKS

9

ALL CREATURES GREAT AND SMALL

OUR home often seemed like a hospital for animals and birds. No creature was too small or insignificant for my father's concentrated care. Here are photographs taken by my mother in that year of the great gales. They were her favourite pictures of my father. He was unaware of the camera at the time and, although his face is partly hidden, his character is revealed far more clearly than it could be in any contrived studio portrait.

His healing gift was not limited to humans. This particular year I watched him with the jackdaws and rooks. It was a year of storm and wind and the plane trees in front of our house bent, tossed and groaned as never before. Putting his car away in the mews garage near our house, he used to come home almost at a run in the evenings, clasping a bowler hat on his head instead of his homburg.

'Chimney-pots are flying: this is the best protection', he would say of the offending hat, as he burst into the house with a gust of wind, hair blown about.

'You look like an undertaker in that hat', my sister said. 'It's hideous', I added.

But the gales continued, and slates blew off the roof, and the hat remained; he was animated as ever at any exciting manifestation of nature.

133

Before long there was mortality in the rookery in the plane trees. A great nest was torn down and the baby birds perished. I have recounted elsewhere how he rescued from a fallen nest a baby rook which had survived, and built a very large wire cage for it in the garden. He fed the little bird four times a day, and thus himself reared it, and kept it until it was strong enough to fly away. But when he took this first rook into his care, it was only the beginning of a story.

Within three weeks, a baby jackdaw had fallen out of a nest in the garden at the back of the house, and when my father heard the raucous agitated squawking from the parent birds, he rushed out of the house and rescued the restless frenzied little creature which could not yet fly and whose wings were damaged. My father's face, I remember, was alight with joy. Another little creature to care for had been discovered. What happiness! He gently and firmly held the bird and carried it down to the great cage to join the baby rook. There was an agitated outburst of croaks and squawks as the two little birds eyed each other. It soon appeared they were not birds of a feather. Pippo, the rook, objected to sharing his home and his master, from whose hand he fed happily every day. Pippo, indeed, had all the instincts of a gentleman, my father used to say. He ate politely and delicately, waiting for a piece of food to be offered to him, and gave tiny affectionate gurgling croaks to my father all the while. Jackie turned out to be a very badly trained little bird, with no nice instincts at all. He would fight for every crumb of food, push Pippo aside, scream in a harsh way to be attended to immediately, and jump up and down on his perch in wild impatience.

It amused and delighted my father to train this rough demanding little creature. He spent every minute of his spare time with the birds, and gradually in some marvellous fashion he communicated his wishes to them, and they fed in turn, side by side on the perch, each taking a morsel as he handed it to first one, then the other, on the pronged stick he had himself specially carved for this purpose. It was not long before another little jackdaw fell out of the nest, and joined the family, and my father was delighted. Feeding them, training them, and really caring for them was a joy to him. But Pippo, the gentle, the loving, remained his favourite. After some months, the cage door was always left open. Jackie and Dora, the other jackdaw, flew away when they were strong enough, and never returned, but Pippo and my father communed and talked to each other for years, and the great rook flew back again and again to trees in the garden or nearby, to call to his master, who never failed to recognise that one bird's cry. In the middle of a meal, my father would leap up, eyes shining, and rush outside, shouting: 'It's Pippo back again'. And the man would gaze into the tree and call gently, as the bird flew right down past him two or three times, uttering the special staccato note he used for my father alone.

It was not only birds for whom he cared. Every sick animal that came to his notice had the same concentrated loving care as his human patients. About this time I was given a small black mongrel dog with short silky coat, big floppy ears, and a ridiculous stump of a tail. Tim became part of life. On the day he was first due to arrive, I flew down the hill from school, satchel flying behind, hair wildly disordered and arrived breathless at the great front door. Ringing the bell impatiently, I opened the letterbox, I remember, to peer through into the hall, wondering if my puppy had come. Presently there was a funny little scuffling pattering sound, and I saw the tiny black rotund form running uncertainly after the maid. Within seconds he was in my arms. What a free simple ecstatic relationship springs up between a child and a pet. It brings out every instinct. Maternal, protective, commanding, tender; for here is an object on which to lavish every pent-up emotion. Loneliness melts away; such, at least, was my feeling.

Within one week my puppy was dying. Tim had contracted distemper at the dog's home where my parents had found him. Dogs were not immunised in those days, and for a puppy to get it so young was almost inevitably fatal. Joy turned to grief and panic. I had given my love irrevocably to a creature who was to be wrested from me almost before we had begun to know each other. Affection so deep, so concentrated, cannot just be laid down at will. Downstairs, in the kitchen where Tim's basket was, I knelt beside my dog who lay there, still and scarcely breathing, hardly even recognising me. I was inconsolable.

It was that evening when my father came home from his round that I poured out my story, begging him to come, to see, to make my puppy better. My father looked very grave, knelt down so quietly beside the limp little form, and began gently to stroke him, fondling his ear, speaking to the puppy as to a creature who must be made to understand that he had come to cure him. He lifted him most carefully, and with extreme gentleness examined his mouth, his ears, sounded his heart with a little wooden stethoscope. I stood beside him in an agony of apprehension. The little dog, who had shown no reaction at all, looked with a strange long look from his dark brown eyes, moved a little, his tail stirred fractionally. It was a response. My father stood up. In two minutes he had everyone flying to carry out his orders.

'Mother, get a thick piece of cloth or soft serge, and machine a coat for this poor little dog, at once.'

He swiftly drew the design for it on paper. My mother was a skilful dressmaker, and she was as anxious as he to save the puppy. The coat was ready in under an hour, I remember. It was navy blue, its edges bound with dark blue braid to make it strong and firm; and there were blue tapes to tie it firmly around him. The cook was asked for a bowl, and boiling water; and out of his surgical stores my father brought cotton wool and disinfectant. Very gently raising the puppy's head, he swabbed out his mouth, trickling the disinfectant down the throat. Every movement was gentle, assured. Now the little dog turned soft loving eyes to my father, sensing, as animals can, the loving concern, the concentrated pouring out of the will to heal.

My father knelt there beside the tiny dog three or four times a day for a week, his hand on that small silky head, swabbing his mouth, feeding him with milk and brandy from a spoon. Only from my father would the dog take nourishment, only for him would he open his mouth to be treated. It seemed like a miracle when, after about a week, my dog suddenly sat up when he saw my father, gave one flying leap out of the basket, raced two or three times round the table in some secret ecstasy of joy as life poured back, and before our astonished eyes raced up the kitchen stairs, and, before anyone could catch him, ran on shaky but oddly swift legs down the great stone staircase into the garden. Round and round he raced, and there my father found him, his little coat twisted and bedraggled, his tongue hanging out, and a sparkle in his eye. He allowed himself to be carried indoors and fed, and he lay down to sleep, exhausted—and well again. His strength soon fully returned and he lived for many years.

There were always stray cats who seemed to know that our doorstep was the right one on which to sit and raise their loud laments. Inevitably they were taken in and found a home. One was gashed in the side, another was wounded in the head, but my father tended their wounds, and they simply stayed and adopted the house, and kept down the mice in the great kitchens and basements.

Because the natural Creation was so full of fascination for my father, he was a biologist of wide knowledge. Often he examined some dead insect under his microscope, and I was called in to notice the marvellous intricacies of pattern and construction. He kept meticulously written notes about any find of interest, studying books on flora and fauna with intense concentration and pleasure, particularly on holiday. Wherever he went, he invariably carried a small pocket magnifying glass, beautifully made, with two lenses. Perhaps such articles as these were his only extravagance. I never saw any other. All his studies had to be in depth. Superficial observations were useless. I often heard him say:

'How anyone can disbelieve the existence of God when you consider the miraculous workings of the smallest insect's frame, I cannot conceive.'

The idea of some sort of evolution was not dismissed by him. Clearly there had been development and progress in all forms of life through aeons of time. But what he refused absolutely to consider was that man had descended from apes. Man, he believed, was a special creation of God, formed for a special purpose, and he alone possessed a loving responsible soul, enabling him to know and respond to his Creator.

I must turn over this page, but it would be easy to linger here, and to live again the moments captured there for ever in the photographs when my father was happy because his rook had flown back to him,—from what distance who could tell? He had given it healing, had seen it fly away, strong and free, and now it came back of its own will and volition, for one reason alone,—love of the man who had given it back its life.

It was freedom that brought life to the bird, gave power to its strong beating wings, and ultimately drew it back, unforced, to see the one who gave it. Had it been kept and guarded in the cage, it would never have known the soaring joy of flight. It might well have died, for the fettered spirit often withers and perishes.

This is a fact that might well be applied on the human level, and perhaps those who try to confine or mould the character of others would do well to consider it. Those who dominate the conscience and thoughts of another too powerfully, deny that very liberty which is life, and may well ultimately find they handle a corpse.

MY MOTHER'S PARENTS

MY GRANDMOTHER AND
MY AUNT

SHE sits rather solemnly beside my sturdy little grandfather as if, like my mother, she is trying to live up to a husband she loves and respects, whose visions are somewhat incomprehensible to her, and this may well have been the case. She is serious, alert, and her dark eyes are somewhat apprehensive. The black Victorian dress, the careful fixed pose suggest that she was photographed on plate somewhere about 1880. The Vicar was a resolute man who spoke up for the underprivileged, preached to his friends the gypsies, loved his family, and thanked God in his diary for his dear wife, his loving little daughters and his tiny son. He died so suddenly leaving his family nearly destitute when two of the children were still at school, that he had almost faded out of memory when I was born. I only occasionally heard him mentioned, and then as someone who was just and kind, and who belonged to a dim past long before the First World War. It was a period which changed the lives and the outlook of many people, imperceptibly but irrevocably, and he belonged to an age which had almost been forgotten.

My grandmother had lingered on into this altered saddened world living in near poverty not far from the parish where her husband had had his ministry. My memory of her is contained in a mental picture of one visit before she died,

141

when I was still very young. She seemed very ancient, and wore a little white lace cap over her white hair; her dress was black. She looked anxiously at us through steel-rimmed glasses, and was lost in our great house. She shrank into a corner of the sofa in the drawing-room as if she did not belong there, and seemed shy and diffident; and I think she was a little in awe of the three maids and the smooth routines of my father's establishment. When she looked at my mother, her eyes were a little sad and longing. I did not know why. She spent her time crocheting. Beautiful and intricate patterns were conjured out of her brain for table runners, edges of table and tray cloths—elaborate formal patterns or tiny shapes of birds and butterflies and flowers. Whenever a meal was announced, she quickly bundled up her work and put it in her little hanging pocket, as if she was afraid she might be late for the descent to the dining-room, where the parlour maid waited to serve the guests, and where we all stood behind our chairs until my father had said grace. Meals at home were formal, the white linen table-cloth was always gleaming and starched, and the silver cutlery shone and sparkled. My grandmother seemed so tiny, so frail, as if the house was too much for her, as if she would like to run away, back to her little pensioner's home where she lived so simply. But I was wrong, as I found out later. There was a consoling strength of character about her that did not reveal itself at first sight.

I always felt she leaned on my mother, and was obviously proud of her. She was gentle to me; I was only a small girl at school, and she always had a warm little questioning smile when I came in. But she felt something much deeper, more complicated for my mother as I found out later. It was my mother who seemed so controlled, so self-sufficient, until I saw her in an unguarded moment, and it was she then who seemed to need someone to lean on. I found it disturbing.

It was on the occasion when my grandmother stayed with us, and my mother went into her room just before she went away. It was a lofty large imposing spare-room. My grand-mother seemed lost in it, and I had thought she did not fit into our house very comfortably. She did not seem at home. I slipped in to say goodbye, then stood shocked and aware, for my mother was clinging to her. They were both in tears.

'I can't bear to leave you, dearie', my grandmother was saying. They seemed to be shaken with deep grief. I did not understand it at all then, and tiptoed quietly out of the room for they were quite unaware of my presence. I think it was not very long after this that she died. I thought of her when the lace-edged tea table-cloths were used in the drawing-room, but my mother hardly spoke of her.

I had two Aunt Marys; and they could hardly have been more different. My father's sister was like a quiet shadow beside my mother's lively uninhibited affectionate younger sister, who also seemed to feel oppressed by our home. She was not academically clever as were her brother, my Uncle George, and my mother. She was a dabbler, in water colours, in the learning of languages, in the keeping of hens, and in the rural life; she had a fly-away inconsequential way of thinking, and did not study any subject deeply. She was devoted to my mother and clearly distracted by the puritan life we led. She must have been quite pretty when she was a slender dark girl with deep brown eyes, who was easily flattered, and loved being the centre of attention. At the end of her life her face was still unlined, her understanding of people still limited, and her disappointments as vivid as a girl's, for she was in some ways immature, in that she lacked the understanding and perception about people that my mother so often displayed.

She conceived it her mission to visit my home from time to

time to 'bring a little gaiety, and brighten you all up, dear,' as she used to explain with alarming determination to my mother. She was married to a rather dour but cheerful Scot of means, who had retired young from shipping to live on his private income. He pottered in his big garden, keeping hens, growing vegetables, and leading an unhurried fairly aimless life.

Whenever a letter from my aunt arrived, hastily scrawled in a large flowing hand, announcing their imminent arrival, my father used to sigh, and a pained look would fleetingly cross his face. My mother always looked a little anxious. Mary was unpredictable. With husband in tow, she would surge into the room with a good deal of exclamation and embracing, and in a determined way would declare her strategy for our 'brightening up'. My mother used almost to flinch.

'Very kind, Mary dear,' she would say, 'but I think . . .'

'No, Louisa, I insist. First, dinner at our hotel tonight. Norfolk duckling is on the menu, I'm told. You shall be our guests.'

She and her husband, much addicted to the pleasures of the table, and the comforts of larger hotels, not unnaturally did not stay in our home which they would have found too puritan for their tastes. However, they always graced us with their presence for tea on the afternoon of their arrival. Various plans of campaign were invariably mooted. We must accompany them to see an art exhibition, drive in the country, go to a concert. But even my aunt, with all her determination, could not lure my mother to the theatre, which in her younger days she had loved. My aunt would employ all her wiles: 'A delightful performance, dear, so educational. In fact it would cheer you all up. Surely that would be permissible?'

The suggestion was always gently turned aside.

But on various occasions my mother took me to stay in her Kentish home, and then could hardly refuse their carefully laid plans to bring 'brightness' into our restricted lives, as they obviously viewed it. This had the astonishing result, one year, of my mother and me being taken to 'a little local show' in Tunbridge Wells. There I watched in amazement a variety show of a somewhat inferior nature, which seemed greatly to please my uncle and aunt. I viewed with surprise a lady clad in silver sequins, who began to divest herself of most of her garments before the undiscriminating audience, to their obvious hearty pleasure. I, who often longed for gaiety, now found I did not like this lady. She did not seem a nice person, I thought, and her motives appeared distinctly dubious. In fact the whole performance seemed tawdry and a little distasteful. Aunt Mary laughed and nodded, and clapped her heavily ringed hands heartily at every act, and tapped her fingers at the music, while Uncle Tony tapped his foot, but my mother sat with a rather frozen look on her face.

The truth was that my mother was more broad-minded and intelligent than my aunt, and I could instinctively sense her pleasure in the best literature, poetry, and drama, which she encouraged me to read for myself as I grew older. Anything really second-rate was distasteful to her. This I sensed, and so I became wary and watchful, and early learned to appreciate what was good. Somehow Aunt Mary's gaiety seemed a little forced, even unnatural to me at times, although I felt a certain sympathy for her marked lack of success in achieving her wishes to 'bring us a little gaiety'.

One year things came to an unexpected climax. My aunt was, I believe, really a most good-natured woman; and I realised, later, she was saddened by my mother's comparatively new puritan streak, and the way in which she had so loyally moulded her life to fit in with that of my father. She would work indefatigably in the attempt to bring her loved sister back into the life of freedom they had both shared. This particular extravaganza, which befell one day, had a totally opposite effect.

The usual letter came, the writing more urgent and flowing than ever. Aunt Mary's arrival was imminent, and she had a surprise in store for us. I looked out of the window that afternoon, saw their car draw up at the door, and a truly astonishing figure climb out. Aunt Mary and her husband vowed they were entitled to wear the Royal Stuart tartan, as my uncle was directly descended, or so they were convinced, from the original Royal Stuart line. Noble blood flowed in his veins, we were told. On occasion, one almost wondered whether he had ideas to be a sort of Pretender to the throne of Scotland. Indeed his hatred of the English government over Scotland was only rivalled by his hatred of Communists. He made up on one occasion a little verse of invective against the importing of butter from the U.S.S.R., and repeated it with relish a number of times at the breakfast table when we stayed with them:

> 'It really is too utterly utter,
> This beastly importing of foreign butter,
> Made by the Bolshies in filthy huts
> And brought over here to poison our . . .!'

In those days the last word was not expressed. Instead he burst into pleased mirth as he reached this point in his rhyme.

On this rather surprising afternoon, therefore, I should not have been as surprised to see my aunt as, in fact, I was. Over the years she had developed a Roman matron's figure. Her proportions, aided, perhaps, by her nightly bottle of stout to maintain her strength, were extremely generous. It was a great shock to see her, then, clad in a bright scarlet kilt, brilliant and arresting in colour, and a tweed jacket tailored to her large and ample figure, descending in full panoply from the car. I turned round, and said unbelievingly: 'She's wearing a bright red kilt.'

My father uttered the nearest thing to an expletive I ever remembered hearing from him, adding,

'IMPOSSIBLE!'

'NO, OH, NO!', said my mother.

I watched Aunt Mary rummage in the back of the car, and draw out an enormous contraption which she slung over her shoulders. She stood erect.

'Mummy, she's got a sort of piano on her front!' I said, in an awed voice. My father took two steps to the window, clapped his hands over his eyes, and said simply: 'I must leave the room!'

My mother, fluttering in anxiety, said: '*What* did you say, dear?'; then went to the window, and staggered back a pace.

'Oh! no, I really can't bear it', she said, half-laughing and gazing blankly at nothing; sinking into a chair, she added in a dazed tone: 'It's an enormous piano accordion. What shall we do?'

My father vanished. The bell rang, the maid opened the door, and my mother went timorously to meet the guests. In walked my aunt, kilt swinging, the swaying piano accordion suspended rather precariously across her bosom. Her beaming face showed that she expected we should be full of delight at this apparition.

'Well, Mary dear, what a surprise!' said my mother in a rather trembling voice, making the understatement of the day.

'Darling', Aunt Mary advanced, and embraced her sister warmly, a little hampered by the accordion, 'I've come to play you some gay tunes on this beautiful instrument which Tony has bought me.'

My uncle beamed at his accomplished wife. He was always indulgent towards her excesses.

She had hardly entered the room when she started to play, feet tapping and moving in time to a Scottish dance tune. Soon she was dancing somewhat skittishly, considering her weight, and I was happily following, for the tune was gay and infectious. The room rocked and shook. My uncle beamed and tapped, and hummed in a harsh throaty under-tone.

My father had mysteriously vanished, and did not put in an appearance for a very long time.

My poor aunt! I believe now that people often failed to fulfil their proper rôles in her life. A regular attender at Matins in the village church where she lived, it was her perpetual grumble that the vicar had never visited her once in twenty years. Perhaps he found her rather formidable. She was a President of the Women's Institute, and quite a figure in the district. A very large woman, she drove an exceedingly small Austin Seven around the village at the extraordinary speed of fifteen miles an hour wherever she went. She was apt to stop haphazardly, issue out in full panoply—the little car often seemed likely to fall apart—carrying parcels, great baskets of eggs, large framed water colour pictures she had painted, and much other parapher-nalia.

But towards the end of her life she and my uncle, soured by long disappointment at the lack of interest in them shown by the Anglican church, became friendly with the Roman Catholic priest. He became a regular and devoted caller at their home. Constant gifts of game from Ireland arrived for them when he was on holiday there. My aunt was deeply touched. A simple lonely woman at heart, childless, deprived to a great extent of the companionship of a loved older sister upon whom she had greatly relied in her youth, she came under the influence of this 'father', and responded avidly to his interest and friendship. Soon she and her husband were persuaded to take instruction, and before long they were both received into the embrace of the Roman Church. My aunt had needed someone to lean on. Here she had found it, and became happy and secure. She had not the strength to remain an outsider in life.

Perhaps it was hardly surprising that at her death, shortly after that of her husband, she should repay this assiduous priest and his Church with almost the whole of a far from inconsiderable estate.

It may well be he deserved it.

It is a matter of regret that my mother's relatives and my father's met each other with so little understanding. Sensitive, vulnerable, kindly, in their differing ways, they appeared to have no point of mutual sensitivity or contact; between them lay fixed a great gulf, and no one was ever able to bridge it.

I I

AUNT EDITH

I NEVER remember seeing my Aunt Edith walk. My earliest
memory is of her lying on a couch in the aunts' small attic
flat. A light rug was draped over her legs, and she had just
come home from London because of ill-health, having had to
give up all her work in connexion with training women missionaries to work in inland China.

She was a stranger to me then, but for the rest of her life
I visited her regularly, and she always talked kindly and
intelligently with a sort of magisterial calm, to the youngest
member of her brother's family. Yet she was in unceasing
pain. The arthritis, which had forced her to give up all active
life, now began slowly, surely, and relentlessly to cripple and
disable her, so that in a few years she became totally unable
to move at all without the help of the nurse attendant who
did everything for her.

It was not long before the couch became the bed. Here, for
thirty years, she lay, gazing out at the small patch of sky
across the vista of roofs and chimney-pots. Perhaps, in retro-
spect she trod those dusty tracks from village to village
outside Chefoo, often sturdily covering the miles on foot, or
else being carried in the Chinese chair suspended on bamboo
poles between two little trotting men, who covered the hard
miles across the wild country. Perhaps she thought of
the women, for whom she had organised educational pro-
jects, had run Bible classes, and whom she had loved. At all

150

events her interest in that far-off land remained undimmed.

As with her sisters, her faith was the staunch unquestioning belief that she had inherited from her father. 'Do you not feel bitter at your illness?' I once asked her when I was growing up. 'I can honestly say that God has enabled me not to be, and has given me peace of mind to endure it', she answered, with her usual disciplined calmness. But I often wondered what thoughts lay beneath that controlled exterior.

Her life had, on the whole, been lived within the framework of the evangelical community, although she was in contact with other denominations as well as the Plymouth Brethren, to whose community she did not, I think, feel exclusively tied. At home the social life of her day left her unmoved, and I think on the whole, disinterested. Nevertheless, she was well informed on current affairs, and a regular reader of *The Times*. But her outlook was entirely missionary: there were people to be won, a faith to proclaim, and a life to live, and in her active days she had been full of tireless zeal in any sphere where duty called.

Perhaps she lacked the warm humour of her brother. Or perhaps, when I knew her, it had been dimmed by suffering, and her strong will had been tempered to an extraordinary stoical acceptance of her total inactivity and ceaseless pain, which she almost never mentioned.

Her main activity lay in the writing of letters, mainly to China, and to her many relatives at home. Indeed I grew to feel that her heart had been left in China, long years before. Her correspondence was the more remarkable in that it caused her great pain even to wield the pen in stiffened arthritic fingers.

Every time I entered her rather drab little bedroom as a child, I felt oppressed. How terrible her plight seemed! Her unfailing quiet welcome, the calm appraising look, and the smile of pleasure at the advent of a visitor, left me feeling that here was a prisoner of circumstance, who exhibited the most iron self-control, and the strictest self-discipline.

What perhaps was significant about my aunt was the unconscious influence she exerted over my home. After all, before the advent of my mother she had been mistress of that home, and had brought up my sisters. It must have been hard for her to accept our presence with equanimity, particularly as my father's life was, after China, the focal point of her interest. Partly, indeed, because of her interests and previous activities, our home sometimes seemed in an extraordinary way to be a sort of outpost of China.

My mother had loyally assumed my aunt's task of holding a monthly prayer meeting for China in our dining-room. It was a day I found depressing. The room took on a very sober character. Chairs were arranged in disciplined rows, and a red hymn-book was placed on each. I used to retire to the nursery, and from the window I watched a number of genteel ladies arrive regularly, to intercede for the needs of that distant land. In wet weather they wore galoshes, and carried large umbrellas, and the hall would be full of their damp mackintoshes. Presently a thin rather melancholy tinkling sound drifted upstairs as they sang a missionary hymn, and then silence fell, and I knew the prayer meeting proper had begun. At the end of the morning, when the ladies had been fortified by tea and biscuits and a little chat, they departed with polite handshakes, and my mother would come upstairs and say with apparent relief, 'Well, it went quite well, I think. Shall we go out and have lunch in the town today?' I came to understand it was her way of reconciling her somewhat difficult tasks with her liking for the bustle and life of the city, and her enjoyment of any chance contacts with friends or acquaintances.

Nevertheless, I also was affected as a child by this extraordinary flavour of China in our home. There were, for example, the beautiful, even magnificent, curios brought to my father from grateful missonary patients; the three Chinese gentlemen for instance. They stood almost two feet high, were made of exquisite coloured porcelain. Their expressions were inscrutable, sinister and remote. There was the ivory Chinese junk, carved with unbelievably intricate detail. There was the carved ivory lion's head with glaring vacant eyes, and a slaughtered ram in its mouth. There were tiny shoes, not four inches long, covered with brilliant coloured silk, made for a Chinese lady in the days when all women's feet were cramped and bound from the days of childhood.

The constant conversations about the needs of China over the dinner table must have inflamed my childish mind, because at one time I became quite obsessed with the thought. I was only about eight years old when I was discovered in the nursery writing down a long list of articles in a clumsy childish hand.

'What are you writing?' asked my mother as I gnawed the pencil, and breathed heavily with the effort of concentrating.

'Things I have to take to China,' I remember answering furtively.

'What have you got to take?' she asked with her usual interest. My reply has inexplicably remained clearly in my memory, and with it the sight of the thick ill-formed letters.

'Matches', I said.

'Why matches,' she asked.

'Because I shall need to burn down all the idols,' I said, with what now seems extraordinary and self-righteous confidence.

But it was the constant arrival at the house of my aunt's missionary friends from China, often as patients to consult my father, that really gave my home its unusual flavour, and set it irrevocably apart from the homes of my friends. Some of the missionaries seemed somehow to live in such a different

THE MISSIONARY

world that there was no communication between us. But two, at least, made an indelible impression on our lives, and became close friends of my mother, and their influence on her cannot be measured, nor would any memories of childhood be complete without some picture of their effect on us.

One of them became so significant in some way to my mother that she took a number of pictures of her.

Here she stands in the garden behind the great house in the Circus, holding up an unfurled scroll covered with Chinese characters. I can see her yet in my mind, powerful, intensely alert, in a way this photograph can only imperfectly suggest. Her dress was slightly flowing, unfashionable, I remember. It did not detract from the strength of her face, or the impact of her character. My mother and I were almost mesmerized by her. I think my mother regarded her as a very great character. A close friendship sprang up between them.

What hold she had over my mother I never knew, but I believe she could have moulded her like putty in her hand, such was the force of her personality. I found her intimidating. Quiet as she was, she had a controlled energy, a leashed dynamic that threatened to pour out over us all and overwhelm us. She was, in that sense, overpowering. Everything about her was positive: the dazzling smile; the boundless energy; the hypnotic power of her words that gripped us as she recounted her unbelievable journeys. The vivid and passionate joy that she seemed to possess for life, for every moment, was centred on her powerful faith. It was the extraordinary intensity of that faith that reached through to me, a child, and I felt as if I was melting away to nothingness in her presence. She was eaten up by some spiritual passion.

Like my aunt in earlier days, she was a missionary from inland China. Her face was aristocratic; her thick wavy hair was as white as snow; her face still showed traces of youth. It was unlined, except for a long scar across her brow. Beside her my mother seemed like a pale candle by a blazing sun.

When I grew older and heard the full story of what had happened to her, I understood why she was in some clear but indefinable way different. She went out as a very young missionary to China, full of vitality, energy and hope. Soon after her arrival in that land, the Boxer risings took place, when many Europeans were massacred by the Chinese brigands, and unbelievable atrocities took place. She was captured with other men and women missionaries, put in a tiny hut without ventilation or sanitation, and left, unable even to lie down or rest. Those there bore their long imprisonment quietly and with all the dignity of true martyrs, for that is what most of them were to become. She was young, full of life and zest and gaiety, and she composed herself to die.

One day her forehead was slashed by one of the brigands as she prayed.

The day appointed for her execution came. She was led outside, thrown down into the mud, and made to lay her head on the block. The brigand raised the flashing sword . . . an eternity passed. She waited for a death that did not come. She was led back to imprisonment. Five times she was led out again to die. Five times, five moments of eternity, she laid her head on the block, and five times the curved sword was raised to execute her . . . five times, utterly inexplicably, all life crammed into the waiting pulsing minutes, the brigand was unable to lower his arm and kill her. So uncanny was this situation, so unbelievable, that the Boxers became highly uneasy; they released her and sent her away, free. She came home to tell the story of how an unseen hand had held back a brigand's arm, and had saved her life.

From that ordeal she emerged white-haired but with one burning purpose, to give all her life, her energies, to the Lord who had so marvellously saved her to do more of His work in that sad and distant land. It was subsequently discovered that at this exact time, groups of Christians, both in England and China, had felt a strange compulsion to pray earnestly for her safety, and unceasingly they had been with her in spirit and in supplication.

'Though I walk through the valley of the shadow of death,
I will fear no evil, for Thou art with me',

she once said with an almost mystical smile. Because of her, this thought came to have a reality that I could understand. It was clear that her faith actually worked. There was a power in it that could not be denied, and she maintained it was a faith that was available for everyone.

What made her different from other people? It was something that she had in common with my father and my aunt, and with many of the people who visited our home. It was something I grew to watch for, to try and assess, and often I envied the assurance of those who shared it. It was the fact that they were the twice-born: they were deeply conscious of their personal acceptance of salvation. Many vowed they could point not only to the day, but to the very hour in which they had 'given their heart to the Lord'. I used to watch them sing with deep and sincere joy the old gospel hymn with its swinging rhythm:

'Oh happy day that fixed my choice
On Thee, my Saviour and my God.'

They were words which carried them away in fervour and emotion, and often, as they sang, their expressions revealed hearts that were 'strangely warmed', even as Wesley's had been. The reality of their relationship with Christ was the most important thing in their lives.

And so, through my aunt's contacts, I had the opportunity of watching a steady stream of people who passed through our home over the years, who were different in their lives and outlook from the people one met in the ordinary traffic of the day, and I immediately recognised them as authentic— for they were people whose lives had an extra indefinable dimension.

I shall always remember the second missionary who had a strong influence over us. We had a rather more varied selection of missionary speakers arriving at our house for big meetings in the city, than did most Plymouth Brethren homes which were restricted generally to those of their own communion. This was due to my mother who rightly insisted on retaining an ecumenical outlook, and who worked indefatigably for various societies, among them the British and Foreign Bible Society and the China Inland Mission. In this connexion, she was adept at gathering large numbers of people in packed meetings in the Guildhall and Pump Room by her tireless method of sending out personal invitations. I think, perhaps, it pleased her to meet Anglican and Free Church clerics, who had a genuine regard for her, and who were glad to use her talents and capabilities as an organiser.

From a very young age, and as soon as I had a clear handwriting, I was roped in to help her address vast numbers of envelopes, summoning the faithful to attend her meetings; and attend they did. The whole operation gained an alarming momentum as the day dawned. The large spare-room was given a special turn-out by the housemaid, and positively reeked of polish and general cleanliness. About lunch-time the speaker generally arrived, a lunch at which conversation was general and courteous; the parlourmaid, as was normal, waited at the table; and then, if the guest was genial, more confidential chit-chat took place with my mother in the drawing-room upstairs. My father would depart to his patients in the consulting-rooms downstairs, and there was a general air of informality. If the guest was rather stiff and shy, my mother generally suggested he or she would like a rest, and everyone retired to take a nap prior to the exertions of the evening.

Miss Mildred Cable and her doughty companion, Miss Francesca French, were much in demand at my mother's great meetings, when, on rather rare occasions, they were home 'on furlough'. Pioneers, explorers, geographers, brilliant writers, these brave intrepid women had travelled in China, Mongolia, Turkestan, and in places where no European had ventured before. It was Miss Cable whom I found fascinating.

One particular year they were to come and speak at a big meeting in the Guildhall, and as usual were staying with us. As always, their visit was an occasion. Somehow they brought an atmosphere of vitality and movement into the house. Their unpretentious little cases, covered with luggage labels from the far quarters of the globe; their sturdy brisk walk indicative of their scorn of the easy life, and their ability to cover great distances by foot, ox-cart, or mule; their direct gaze which looked at and through you piercingly but compassionately; their total indifference to the trivia of life, but their alert minds which drew you into their interests and enthusiasms; all these things made them unusual but loved visitors. They were used to braving hardship undreamed of by normal people in the society which surrounded but did not really penetrate my home, which itself, of course, was a sort of rocky islet in the soft waters of worldly prosperity and ease around us.

It so happened that it had always been my great desire to be in a school play; the lure of the footlights burned strong in one small puritan's heart, but my father would not allow this, for as has been told the very word 'stage' filled him with unreasoning antipathy. Somehow I grew used to this deprivation, which, like others in my life, was softened by his love and concern for one's welfare, and his sympathy when life was hard. Yet very occasionally I felt sadness and shed bitter tears, but only in secrecy. I did not want to be pitied: it was preferable that one should not show one's feelings in this matter. It would have been almost worse to hear a good man harshly criticised, for I loved my austere father. Indeed I sometimes reached a willingness to 'give up' something for the sake of one's faith, and if, lamentably for me, it must be a part in a play, then like a true puritan's daughter I must do it willingly. Such exalted moods, however, were rare. Often the subject was sore within me.

Quite suddenly, for me, with the advent of Miss Cable that day, a dramatic and unexpected event occurred. Miss Cable, as usual, was sitting erect and forward in a corner of the big sofa. Little white-haired woman as she was, her face was one of the strongest and most compelling that I had ever seen. So when she bent her full concentration suddenly upon me, I was—as ever—gripped and fascinated, and I gazed back at her questioningly and eagerly. Some emotion was burning in her eyes, which were deeply kind and searching. She drew me to her, put an arm around me, and talked confidentally as if she and I were alone in the great room, and I listened agog:

'Anne', she said, 'I wonder if you would do something very special for me tonight?'

I could not imagine what she had in mind, and was filled with curiosity, and apprehension.

'We would like you to dress up tonight and take the part of a little Mongolian girl', said Miss Cable. I could hardly believe what I was hearing.

'We have brought the clothes from China with us,' she continued, 'and you will hide behind the platform with Miss French, and at a given word will walk forward in these clothes, and I shall introduce you to the audience, and describe the life of such a child, so that they may picture the scene better. Will you do this for me, Anne?'

Would I do it? A breathless excitement seized me: dress up, impersonate someone, step out onto the stage, for it was as good as a stage, face hundreds of people with Miss Cable whom I loved—for love and gratitude were pouring into my heart; why, it was heaven! I would be in my own one-act, two-person play, I who had been denied any part in a school dramatic performance. But this was worth them all. I nodded, speechless. Somehow, I believe that Miss Cable, that most perceptive of women, understood a little of the excitement she had engendered in my heart. I could hardly wait for the evening to come.

Highly excited, I prepared for my 'part'. I had a seat in the special taxi taking the suitcase with my Mongolian garments, Miss Cable, Miss French and me to the Guildhall. Full of importance I tiptoed behind Miss French in conspiratorial manner, past the great crowds, up onto the platform, where Miss Cable joined the clerics and the prominent laymen who had come to do her honour. I sat beside a little door opening off the back of the platform, wherein the suitcase was placed, in a tiny room—my dressing room! Never had a missionary meeting taken on this colourful aspect. I gazed down at the sea of expectant faces, and a thrumming piano broke into suitable warming-up music.

At a given moment, the great meeting opened, with a paeon of praise, and I joined in, as the audience rose and the swelling chords broke into the splendid triumphal tune of

> 'Jesus shall reign where'er the sun
> Doth his successive journeys run;
> His kingdoms stretch from shore to shore,
> Till moons shall wax and wane no more.'

My throat was tight; the excitement nearly choked me.

When eventually, after the first part of the meeting was over, Miss Cable rose to speak, small and still, the great hall became intensely silent: the hush was palpitating. There was a captivating and compelling warmth and interest in her clear voice; like silver bells it fell on a child's hot and eager brain. It was always so with her. She held the audience in the palm of her hand. I became so enthralled, gazing out in amazement over the grey and sandy wastes of the Gobi desert, that I almost forgot my part. But Miss French suddenly seized me, and pushed me through the little door; trembling from head to foot, I was arrayed in an astonishing white garment of embroidered cotton, with slits only for the eyes. It covered me from head to toe, and I must have appeared like a rather ornate member of the Klu Klux Klan. Miss French opened the door a crack, put her ear to it and we waited what seemed an interminable time, and I heard the voice of Miss Cable as she continued her story. Suddenly Miss French stiffened, stood upright, opened the door and gave me a little push. I felt as if I was about to faint as I heard Miss Gable say in a welcoming voice, half turning to look behind her:

'Now I have brought a little Mongolian girl to see you, so that you can picture her in your minds . . .'

Another push from Miss French, and I advanced, smiling rather fatuously through the slits, and went to the front of the platform to take up my position beside Miss Cable. I must have looked strange, and 'Oohs' and 'Aahs' broke out from the warm-hearted audience. To my amazement this turned into a soft and appreciative clapping, and my cup was full. Miss Cable took my hand, pointed out strange features of the costume, sketched an imaginary day in my life, stressed the fears and griefs of such a child, and eventually having stirred her audience to real depths of interest, emotion and sympathy, finished.

The audience, as always, moved and disturbed, rose to the thunderous notes of the last hymn, and 'From Greenland's icy mountains' echoed through the Guildhall in surges of sound that rolled over my excited and bemused head.

Thus ended my first and only 'stage' appearance during childhood.

As I think back to those unusual characters whom I met, the outstanding memory I have of them as of my aunt, is their courage. It is exemplified in the memorable travel book, *The Gobi Desert*, written by Mildred Cable with Francesca French. In it Miss Cable describes their first view of the desolate wastes of the Gobi, as they looked out at it from the North West Wall of China, before they began their epic journey to carry the Christian gospel to those who had never heard it. 'A place of desolation', one of them remarks. A Chinese soldier standing nearby warns them of its perils, and seems horrified at the temerity of three women setting out on such a foolhardy journey. Many get lost in the desert, he warns them, adding 'some miss their way and die of thirst, and others are frozen to death in winter blizzards. You do not yet know, lady, the terrors of that journey. Must you go out into the Gobi? . . .' Miss Cable's simple answer remains like a beacon in the mind:

'Yes, I must, for I seek the lost, and some are out there.'

My copy of the book is a little worn now, as it is one of my treasured possessions. Perhaps it was because she had a deep understanding both of my family and of a child who was full of hopes and fears, and also because she knew the conflicts such a home as mine could cause, that she later wrote in her own hand on the front page a sort of parting message to me to carry through life:

'The desert shall blossom as the rose!'

12

SUNDAY

THE thought of fishing was to become part of the background of my life, for I lived among those whose great desire was to be 'fishers of men.' This was the divine command, this was the mission specifically laid down for them in the gospels.

I was able to watch many of them at work, for every Sunday I vanished from the company of friends and companions and became a 'meeting child'. The separation between the happiness of weekdays and the rigidity of Sunday's routines often seemed divisive. For the disciplines of this particular form of upbringing were strict, and were enforced wherever we were. Somehow this marked us out as subtly different. All the week we might appear the same as other people. But on Sundays we were separated like the sheep and the goats, and we departed into the camp of the small unpopular minority, or so it then seemed. It was the same wherever we went.

In the summer holidays it was in Devonshire. The sunny weekdays were so happy. The sea called to me. I used to listen to the eternal restless sound of the foam-crested waves that crashed against the steep banks of shingle. As I lay on the hard limpet-studded surface of the rocks, I gazed down into deep shaded pools. Long probing shafts of sunlight warmed the translucent water in the deep crevices, penetrating the darkness, and revealing little red sea anemones fringed like petals of strange exotic flowers, and lighting up tiny silvery fish as they darted swiftly from secret hiding-

places, and flashed and circled in the water, vanishing as
quickly as they had come. Overhead the gulls flew to and
fro. Sometimes they sailed down onto a nearby rock, and
stood looking at me out of solemn unwinking yellow eyes.
Then with long echoing cries they soared up again, drifting
through the golden air. Sometimes I stood barefoot beside
the fishermen at the edge of the sea. I was allowed to haul on
the thick, wet sticky rope at each end of their U-shaped net,
marked in the sea by its bobbing cork floats; it was drawn in
by two groups of men some hundred yards apart. The rope
grazed the hands, but there was the eager anticipation of
seeing the catch, and the gulls swooped and cried, as very
slowly we pulled and strained. The heavy rope coiled and
dropped behind us as the men on each side heaved and
dragged, their heels jammed down into the shingle, while
they all leaned back with their weight on the rope pulling it
steadily in, hand over hand, in rhythmic movement. Then
came the moment for which all waited. The gulls wheeled,
their cries rising to a crescendo. Leaping into the sunlight,
the whitebait came in, little flashing silvery darts of light
which mingled and whirled, their tiny bodies hitting the
water in a frenzy of hissing movement, as they tried to escape
the voracious shoals of mackerel behind. As the net drew in
to the shore, a great harvest of fish was leaping and splashing
in the sunlight at the edge of the sea, and the mackerel
hurled themselves frenziedly into the air, falling and gasping
as they were dragged from their native element. Everyone
crowded around the net. Dark blue crabs and lobsters,
crawling, pincers waving, were firmly seized and packed
alive into great baskets. The mackerel, a shimmering mass,
their silver, blue, and green bodies writhing and twisting,
were pushed into stained wooden boxes. Overhead the gulls
still called restlessly to each other. I was sometimes given
two live mackerel by a smiling fisherman, who stuck my

inexpert fingers into the gills, which still opened and shut faintly. I felt like a murderer as I carried them home for supper, and every now and then they gave a last desperate tremor and a convulsive gasp.

On Sundays I sat in the little red brick meeting hall, not far from the sea, and I listened to different sounds. I can still hear them. The rough voices of the Devon fishermen singing their gospel hymns come echoing down the years. Standing there in stiff Sunday suits and starched white collars instead of their weekday dark blue jerseys, stained serge trousers and rubber boots, they sang with a fervour and a certainty about their faith. During the reading of the Bible they sat formal and quiet, while one of their number, the leading brother, a red-faced elderly man with crisp wavy iron-grey hair, often read from the Book of Revelation. His large leather Bible was well thumbed, the pages thin and blurred at the edges with a life-time's constant reading. Many verses were carefully underlined. His voice had a husky softness, and the great echoing words used to rise and fall like the sighing of the sea:

'And I heard as it were the voice of a great multitude, as the voice of many waters, and as the voice of mighty thunderings, saying "Alleluia, for the Lord God omnipotent reigneth".'

While the Brethren listened to the majestic words, a sigh, almost imperceptible, passed from one to another, as they filled their hearts with the wonders of the Lord. Sometimes, as they spoke their direct extempore prayers, talking in their own language to their Maker, one or another would utter a fervent 'Amen', or 'Hallelujah, praise the Lord'. Honest and sincere, they looked into one's eyes with alert almost cold blue eyes that seemed to reflect the colour of the sea, eyes that were used to scanning the ocean for the coming of

mackerel, or the approaching storm. There was a rough and
joyful sweetness as they sang the old chorus: 'I will make you
fishers of men'. It was language they understood.

At home in Bath, Sundays had the same flavour. Divorced
entirely in character from weekdays, they yet moulded and
coloured the whole of life. I felt unlike other children. I was
really an outsider from the life of my friends. In this setting I
sometimes chafed at the strict disciplines my father imposed.
I fought his strictures, and wept in secret at his rules. But his
love and his sincerity I could never question, and at last I
learned to accept silently the keeping of the Sabbath. It was
not an exciting day. No secular reading was allowed, although
I frequently broke this rule by vanishing into my bedroom.
No activity was undertaken except the most simple: walking,
attending the various meetings, reading something of a
special nature, painting Bible pictures, searching for texts for
a competition in a religious magazine. Oddly, as it now seems,
I believe it was very restful. The brain literally lay fallow for a
whole day. I believe I spent hours daydreaming, and unconsciously absorbing the matchless poetry and prose of the
Authorised Version.

For my father, Sunday was the climax of his week. It was
his time of renewal, a time when, in spirit, he entered a holy
place, temporarily laying aside problems and anxieties. I
believe there was something of the mystic in him. His astonishing vigour, and powers of recuperation from illness or
weariness stemmed from this ability to retreat inwards and
look upwards. His 'Sunday face' glowed with an inner happiness.

Each Sunday morning and evening I sat beside him in the
meeting whenever he was not called out to sick patients, and
I allowed the thoughts of those with whom he worshipped to
flow over me. I learned something from this discipline, for
like most of the children there I learned to relax and forget

tensions during the long period of stillness and quiet. Immediately I entered the hall, I felt as if I had entered another world hidden away from the eyes of all who knew us. The black and white notice, 'Gospel Hall', hanging in the street outside indicated our 'apartness' from others, and this always bred a conflict in the mind. For I used to ask myself why, why, were we not able to go to any church or any chapel, but only the meeting. No answer ever satisfied me.

When the baize doors were pushed open, and we entered the warm hall, I was immediately aware of stillness in a place that was full of people sitting with bowed heads or open Bibles on their laps. It was a tight-knit community. The elder brother at the door gripped one's hand, smiling in genuine pleasure. The Brethren felt real love and concern for each other, and their eyes glowed with quiet pleasure when they met. This makes the sadder the constant astonishing and barren divisions that arose through the years among certain of them over practices and principles of gathering in many of their meetings. These split them into many mutually exclusive groups. The appalling spectacle of people who call themselves Christians actually refusing to eat with members of their own family holding different beliefs, is the disastrous culmination of a heretical pharisaism today among one section of those who have become known as the Exclusive Brethren.

But as a child brought up among the more liberal Brethren, I was unaware of the divisions. Certainly I did not like being different from my friends, but I felt the genuine affection of those who met in the hall. In the alcove where we sat under a large window with small square panes, I used to watch the people around me. My mother studied her Bible with a slight frown of concentration on her intelligent face. She was the eternal student at heart, an academic who thirsted for knowledge. She applied her keen intellect to the study of Old

Testament history. I surmise she often pursued some find,
some unexpected detail revealing a hidden insight into her
conclusions. As a mathematician she could not be vague or
inconclusive. She liked to consider facts, and interpret their
significance. It was for this reason, I think, that she took up as
a hobby the study in depth of Biblical archaeology, reading
endless tomes, examining evidence, weighing theories. She
became fascinated, finding proofs of the truth and accuracy
of the scriptural accounts of the history of the Israelites, and
writing popular articles for evangelical journals. They were
far more lively that many others I have seen. I grew accustomed to hearing enthusiastic conversations at the lunch or
dinner table, when she and my father relentlessly pursued
many a happy discovery or train of thought, rejoicing in its
significance, and in its proof of the astonishing accuracy of
Scripture. Names like Asshur Banipal, Tiglath Pileser,
Nefertiti, were bandied over my head, and it was some time
before I was aware such topics were slightly unusual. Generally she surreptitiously stuffed a few sheets of notepaper into
her Bible, and very quietly she used to employ the time in
the stillness of the meeting by jotting down a few pencil notes.

My father was of a different calibre. I used to watch him
kneeling there, week by week, on the hard bare boards of the
floor in the gospel hall, rapt and carried away as he turned
his whole heart towards God. Most of the Brethren remained
seated during prayer. My father always knelt. His singleness
of heart was, to ordinary people, unintelligible. He was an
enigma. But I was aware that I lived beside a man whose
faith was more powerful than that of almost anyone I knew.
I was aware that even the smallest detail of his day was subjected to divine scrutiny. Everything was submitted to the
test of 'If the Lord wills'. The words were both a silent
standard, and a spoken comment, and they were often uttered as naturally as if he had said, 'If the weather is good'.

I was often drawn to the kindly middle-aged 'sister' who sat in front of me. She came of a cultured wealthy family who had entered the Brethren movement in Victorian days. Those who remained in it were gentle pietists. Those who had left it soared in their professions and vocations to high academic and professional positions. This was a pattern I was to see repeated frequently. Perhaps it was the strong faith and iron disciplines, never wholly forgotten, that produced in them a forcefulness and independence of outlook that blended into a powerful dynamic. Emancipated Brethren have always had a sturdy ability to stand alone. They have had to learn this in a hard school, for in many cases they have remained 'outsiders'; for while they are able to enter many differing social groups and strata of society, they *belong* wholly to none. In leaving the environment in which they grew up, they have torn up roots, which may not easily be planted again.

My memories of this gentle 'sister' are connected with my deep disgrace one summer Sunday morning. Often, in the close heat, I seemed to become immutably stuck to the dark wooden seat, pitted and scratched a little through age, but regularly polished into a dark gloss. As the warm sunbeams slanted through the window beside us, we were surrounded by a myriad shifting dancing particles of dust, transformed into whirling golden specks. She sat imprisoned in a brilliant glow on the bench in front of us. Her smooth neat bun at the nape of her neck, her glossy broad-brimmed brown hat with two dangling cherries on one side, were bathed in a halo of light. I found the long dissertation of one of the elder Brethren very tedious. The fervent words, which seemed to have little bearing on daily life, floated away in the close atmosphere. It was astonishing how fluently the Brethren were able to express their thoughts. I think they must often have stored up the fruits of a week's meditation ready to give us the benefit of it, if opportunity occurred. With no preparation they could turn from passage to passage in the Bible with swift ease, noting likenesses and allusions between different books, and finding parallel meanings between the Old and New Testaments. Leviticus was particularly fruitful. I was, I remember, much exercised about 'the caul' that day. It appeared it had some spiritual significance. I was far more anxious to discover what it actually was. As I puzzled, I grew increasingly restless. I shifted up and down on the sticky seat, finding it impossible to keep still. Warning looks from my mother, pained looks from my father, failed to quell the ardent desire to move. Suddenly I felt an alarming vice-like grip on my left wrist. My father's patience was at an end. He was, to put it clearly, exasperated. Firmly and severely he removed me to his other side on the outside edge of the seat, an outcast who was disturbing those who were wrapped in meditation. It was no good. I was not quietened. I dropped my hymn-book with a loud clatter onto the floor, bent down to retrieve it, glad of the excuse to stretch my limbs, and quite suddenly lost my balance. I fell on my head upside down on the drab linoleum in the aisle between the seats, conscious only that my legs had shot up in the air, and I was doing a sort of handstand. From my inverted position I gazed up aghast to see my special hated Sunday undergarment,—white frilled cotton knickers—alarmingly displayed before the eyes of the Saints. It was a terrible moment. I was hauled back into my seat in deepest ignominy, and knew I could not face my father. But suddenly from my middle-aged friend on the seat in front there came a little burst of suppressed laughter, and she put her lace handker-chief, smelling of lavender over her mouth, and I saw her shoulders shaking. From that moment there was a bond between us which lasted through the years.

I often felt sorry for her, and wondered why she had never married. Was there, I asked myself, no suitable Plymouth

Brother with whom she might have found quiet solace. True, the choice was not unlimited. She had a gentle merriment, and her expression of natural liveliness was tempered to an almost unnatural serenity. She spent her days doing good works, and lived alone in a quiet stone house on one of the hills in Bath. Here she sometimes gave us tea out of beautiful bone china, with a discreet flower pattern in soft colours. Her drawing-room was full of graceful antique furniture, On her piano lay all the evangelical hymn-books. Often she seemed to overflow with affection, embracing my mother and me with a sort of loving understanding of our unexpressed needs, and her searching eyes looked into ours, to see, I think, if she saw happiness there.

She was, I believe, far more perceptive, and broader in outlook than some of those in our meeting, who seemed strangely unconscious of the world around them. Some had come in adult life to this group of people, not having previously fitted into any church or chapel happily, for they failed to find satisfaction where fundamental doctrines were less strongly presented. Their presence was often proof of a faith hard won and now held with what must be called passion. Those who, on the other hand, had lived in the Brethren setting for most of their lives, obstinately rejected the validity of any denomination or sect, or any form of worship other than their own. Some said, almost with pride, 'We have left the sects'; and, in a sort of isolation they pursued the puritan routines and the basic Bible truths oblivious of the life of any other church. It was as though they had shut themselves in a small room, in which there was a great telescope trained directly towards the heavens. No intruder was allowed to disturb their concentrated contemplation. No intermediary was permitted to interpret what they saw. Their eyes were fixed on God, and life as it flowed by outside their observatory was irrelevant.

This withdrawal from the world might be considered strange in those who would have said their first task was to 'fish' for the souls of men. I believe this contradiction was the sharper in that they often did not communicate in the language of those who lived around them. Their speech was sometimes archaic, often Biblical, for the words of Scripture flowed naturally from their lips, forming their thought patterns and the basis of their convictions. Sometimes it was dignified, beautiful. 'Sit still, my daughter', my father said on occasion, in the language of the Book of Ruth, when he was attempting to instil serenity into my restless heart; and somehow, the words were relevant. But it seems so clear now that the Christian faith needs to be expressed in the language of the present as well as preserved in the speech of the past, if it is to have contemporary relevance. The Hebrews in the centuries before Christ wrote matchless poetry. They showed exceptional qualities of listening for divine revelation. They accepted moral disciplines that mean nothing today. But to pass on the inspiration and the wisdom of the Bible means that it must not only be translated into relevant contemporary terms but it must also be expressed in the idiom of the day to those who have no knowledge of Christian belief.

Sunday brought not only the discipline of quiet in the morning meeting, but also the challenge of 'the sound of the gospel', which in every Brethren hall is faithfully proclaimed each Sunday night as well as at other times. The evening meeting was as much, perhaps even more, part of the fabric of my life, as was the Sunday morning quiet meditation. It was certainly in every sense more disturbing. The whole presentation of the gospel of redemption was slanted towards unequivocal acceptance. Although at school we were trained to discuss and consider a problem, it appeared that in matters of faith I must acquiesce without questioning. Later, I grew to feel that the tackle of these 'fishers of men' needed a radical overhaul. Very few strangers or 'unconverted' people ever came to the hall. Yet the Brethren waited hopefully, expectantly, for some heavy catch that never came to their net, apparently believing that if the gospel were 'offered', and proclaimed each Sunday, much of their task was completed. Such a situation is clearly apparent in many churches today. Yet the best fish are often found in the most turbulent waters, and our Lord emphasised clearly the need for launching into the deep. Certainly the Brethren were very active in missionary work overseas. But their lives at home were totally different from those of the people living around them.

For me, the Sunday gospel meeting became the central problem in life. It bred anxiety and confusion of mind, all because I began to wonder if I was saved. At first I enjoyed going to it because of the harmonium. For reasons I could never fathom, there was no instrumental accompaniment on Sunday mornings. But in the evening, the large wheezy harmonium with its swelling notes and thrumming cadences caused me intense pleasure. In fact the whole evening was connected in my mind with sound and clangour. For as we walked to the gospel hall, we used to hear the joyous beat of the great drum and tambourines of the Salvation Army band, whose members walked with swinging steps and heads lifted high down the narrow decayed streets near our hall. I could happily have danced to their music. The bells of the Abbey, too, would join in the clamour as they summoned the faithful to Evensong nearby, and sometimes I wished we could join those who were inside, for dimly through the great doors came the muted cadences of rolling organ music.

Swallowed up in the quiet of the meeting hall I was aware of the peaceful atmosphere of hope and trust, free from troublesome doubts, which is so strong a mark of the Brethren's gatherings. It seemed to accentuate my own uncer-

tainties. Yet, like others, I was stabbed by the greatest story
in the world, and my restless spirit, yearning for drama, got
it, as the great pictures unfolded in stark majesty. Vivid,
horrifying, unspeakably beautiful, they were imprinted for
ever in the mind of a child.

For a hush would fall upon those sitting there, and the
brother chosen to speak that night would rise to his feet and
give out a hymn that I still cannot hear without emotion:

> 'There were ninety and nine that safely lay
>   In the shelter of the fold;
> But one was out on the hills away
>   Far off from the gates of gold'.

It was a familiar picture. In various Bible story books given to
me by numerous relatives, and thought suitable for my instruction, I had gazed at illustrations of Eastern shepherds
leading their flocks across barren stony lands. But I always
turned the pages quickly to find the page where the lost
lamb was hopelessly caught in a thicket of thorns. Lost, left
behind by the flock, trembling under a dark and stormy sky,
I seemed to be looking at a pictorial representation of myself, the one who was also so likely to be left behind. How
poignant, then, was the next picture of the great central
character of the shepherd leaning forward, straining and
stretching towards the little lamb over a desperate rocky
ravine, in very peril of his life. How vividly I saw it all as we
sang the old hymn. I watched in my mind the shepherd
move fearlessly into cruel danger.

> 'But none of the ransomed ever knew
>   How deep were the waters crossed,
> Nor how dark was the night that the Lord passed
>   through
>   Ere he found his sheep that was lost.'

So I sat there, rapt, carried away; sad yet hopeful; anxious

yet consoled; an ordinary child with imperfect understanding, and deep longings. Some of the words of the hymn were
hackneyed. It did not matter. My mind was fed on strong
meat: on the great biblical thoughts of sorrow and joy; of
rejection and acceptance.

After the meeting was over, my father and I left our seats,
and he would nod and smile to one and another, and propel
me gently past the little groups of 'saints' chatting comfortably together. This somewhat surprising term did not,
in fact, have any reference to their righteousness. It was the
biblical word used of believers in Christ in the Acts of the
Apostles when Paul called the members of a new church,
for example, 'the saints at Corinth'.

If some particularly happy thought had occurred to my
father during the reading of the Scripture preceding the
preaching of the gospel, he would often feel moved to tell one
of the elder brethren about it after the service, and gripping
him by the elbow he would draw him aside, his face alight
with a real joy as he contemplated the things of the spirit. I
would stand and shift from foot to foot impatient to be away.
These devotional thoughts were above my head. I sensed that
I was almost forgotten by my father in his absorption in his
subject, and I knew those there listened to him with respect.

Eventually, remembering I was beside him, he would
break off his spiritual discourse, and the warm smile would
cross his face as, half-apologetically, he would say, 'Well, old
lady, you've waited long enough, I think'. Then detaching
himself from his conversation, he would bow briefly to
indicate it was finished, and we would pass down the hall
past the little groups of people to the dark stone-flagged
porch and the open door where the night air was drifting in.

One cold and frosty night we came out of the hot brightly-
lit hall, whose steamed up windows had cosily enclosed us
from the world outside, while those within had happily and

confidently sung the songs of salvation, and we stepped out together into the winter night.

Glad to be free of the hard seat, I stretched my legs, and half danced along the old paved street beside my father, under the gas lamps which cast a melancholy pool of light across the path. My father was oblivious of what I was doing, and I saw him gazing up past the street light, his eyes fixed on the tattered dark clouds edged with silver as they raced past the moon. He loved to watch the heavens. Then he took my hand again, and tightening his grip, as he always did when there were urgent things to say, he began: 'Darling, when we remember how our Lord died for us on the cross at Cavalry, and endured much suffering for our sake, how terrible it must be to turn our backs on Him and to reject His love, when He is waiting to give us His wonderful gift of eternal life.'

Then gazing down at me, he added quietly: 'Each one of us is free, you know. The choice is ours alone.'

Silence fell dreadfully between us. I saw his expression longing, even wistful. I knew it was my future about which he was concerned, my soul's salvation for which he longed. He was fishing in deep waters to bring in his child, and the bait must be a challenge and a choice.

He was concerned, too, to cast the net farther and bring in those who never came to the Sunday services other than the close-knit members of the group. So from time to time he urged the Brethren to go out more, to seek farther for those in need, 'the lost' in Biblical terminology. He urged them to have regular open-air services in the downtown parts of the city. It was in this act which arose from his concern for men, that my father caused acute distress in his own family. How sharply came a sword among us then, sinister, wounding, and who was there to heal the scars?

One Sunday he got up from the table, and said he must

join the little gathering to be held in the open air at a street corner that evening. There was silence. I could see it all; they would set up the small harmonium, hand out to any hesitant passers-by the red hymn books, *Redemption Songs and Solos*, a title which I think cannot have had much meaning for the man in the street; and the little group of people, rather soberly dressed, would gather round bravely to sing the songs of Zion:

> 'Saviour, if of Zion's city
> I through faith a member am . . .'

I do not believe many paused to listen to them. But if one soul could be reached, their happiness was complete. It was one of my sisters who, that night, was tormented with distress when my father declared his intention of going to take his stand beside them, and to preach the gospel of Christ.

He could not see it, but it was, I am convinced, love for him that tortured her, and threatened to destroy their relationship. How well I grew to understand her emotion.

'You, a leading consultant, one of the best doctors in this city, to go and stand up and preach with that odd little set of people who haven't a conception of what ordinary people are like! How *can* you? You will make yourself look a fool; eccentric; you will be laughed at, despised. And what will my friends think? Their fathers never make an exhibition of themselves.'

She was tormented, wanting to shield him from the scorn of the world. But my father was happy, as was St. Paul, to be a fool for Christ's sake if need be. He was wounded at her words, felt himself condemned in her eyes, and walked away alone, sad and silent, to take his stand by the creaking harmonium; and he believed that his own children scorned him.

But it was my sister who was inwardly weeping. It is hard

to have your father mocked, laughed at, talked about with a slight curl of the lip. She knew it all so well. She could not bear that a man of his outstanding healing power should be condemned for his eccentricities. Perhaps secretly she felt his action betrayed her. If her father could expose her to the secret ridicule of friends, then what love was in him? Did she feel this? I do not know, but the rift in understanding between them arose from a passionate concern for each other, and neither could see it. It seemed then as if something evil was born out of goodness. Where healing might be found I could not tell.

UNCLE HARRY

13

UNCLE HARRY

THERE was one person who could bridge the turbulent waters of conflicting viewpoints in my unworldly home. It was my Uncle Harry who was the most harmonising influence we knew, perhaps because he loved my father and was prepared to accept him exactly as he was. He treated him without any self-consciousness or preconceived ideas. It was he who had married my father's younger sister, Margaret, in face of strong opposition from his parents, for they were first cousins. But their happiness together, and their easy relationship had enabled them to make a satisfying life. He was an integrated personality, a man of affairs, about whom there was an indefinable air of distinction. A banker, he was a partner in Childs' Bank at 1, Fleet Street, and over the years through his flair for investments, he became a man of great property. He seemed to me to have a certain air of authority, yet, as I remember, he never raised his voice except in laughter.

He looks at me now from this portrait photograph, and he is just as I knew him when I was about twelve or thirteen years old. The thick silvery hair frames a lean face, very slightly furrowed. He is clean-shaven except for the grey moustache; and his blue eyes with their slightly quizzical look have a benevolent whimsical expression, but also much shrewdness. I am inclined to think that he saw far more than he ever revealed. He was pre-eminently a man of peace, something of a diplomat who drew out harmony, not discord, in the symphonic variations of human relationships, so he was a musician by instinct, and also in fact. To the world of today he might have looked like a Forsyte figure, dressed always in impeccable taste, unostentatious but clearly expensive. This is seen in his portrait. The wing collar, the grey silk tie, the diamond horseshoe head on his gold tie-pin, and the style of the well-cut Bond Street grey suit, all suggest that the time was in the 1920s. Those were the years when I knew him best, and when he came regularly to stay in our home, where he exerted an indefinable healing influence over us all.

You could say that nearly all of my family had this taste, this desire for a faith, perhaps for different motives, or because of various needs, and perhaps because, whatever their differences, they were sincere people with a measure of humility, and knew that to be alone in the human situation with nothing to hold on to, nothing in which to believe, would be such nihilism, such despair, that it was not to be considered. They were thinkers, some in limited channels, some ranging across distant uncharted seas, and all were prepared to put their most searching efforts towards the discovery of a life-style. For most of them it was the conviction of the truth of the Christian faith that was to carry them strongly, steadily, through their days. I think my uncle held his beliefs no less firmly than my father. But he allowed them to blend, not to clash with his environment. Was this an easy way out? I often wondered.

I had to admit, as I later considered this question over the years, that the rugged saints of history have always been awkward figures, who threw down the gauntlet to their generation, challenging and disturbing them. Like a pebble thrown in a deep lake, their influence has stretched out in ever-widening circles, reaching undreamed-of distances.

They were people who were hard to live with, uneasy to hear, yet their voices have echoed down chasms of thought in the minds of men long after they have gone. It has always been easy to ignore them, unless there has been an answering echo in the heart, a spark of recognition leaping up as dry tinder to flame when they spoke. When I grew older, I slowly came to realise that, although his path could not wholly be mine and was therefore not always easy to accept, my father showed something of their calibre.

My uncle had not, perhaps, the intensity of faith that my father had. But together they were walking the same road. It did not seem to matter to them that one walked over sharp-edged stones, while the other chose the softer grass at the edge of the track. Neither grudged the other his position. They were looking in the same direction, and this was all that mattered.

I was envious of the difference between them, of the fact that my uncle's establishment Christianity—for he was a sincere and practising Anglican, given secretly to doing much good—made life so happy for his family. There was no conflict in that home; it was at peace.

It was odd that I never felt for Uncle Harry the warm love I had for Uncle George. I was fond of him, admired his easy diplomatic approach to the contrasting characters in my home who, like sharp uncut flints, rubbed against each other so uneasily from time to time. Uncle Harry could charm my sisters as my father never could. In his world they were happy. Who could blame them? When he walked off the London train as it drew around the curved track into the station, he came towards us with that light springing step so like my father's, his homburg slightly tilted, pipe in mouth, and an expensive hide suitcase in one hand. He had only to step among us for my father to be overjoyed at the sight of him:

'My dear old boy.'

'Well, my dear fellow . . .'

and my sisters also were at peace. The two men used to grasp each other's hands, their eyes shining with unaffected pleasure. How different they were! I think now they drew a strange strength from each other's opposite qualities.

Why then could I not have the same feeling for this uncle who was so humorous, so accepting of the foibles of our family, as I did for my mother's brother? It was, I think, because my mother and I were comparative newcomers to a scene whose background had been painted in strong dark colours long before we came. It was a place whose mountains and valleys had been charted before our time, where my uncle had shared joys and sorrows with those who belonged there. He had walked by my father since boyhood; had seen him in grief and loneliness; had known his children motherless and had given them solace. It was natural: we had arrived too late on the scene to be relevant to it. We were, in a sense, intruders. The timing of my arrival had been unfortunate and he knew it. With all his kindness, my uncle did not need us. My mother's brother did. Yet it was Uncle George who could find no bridge over which he might cross to us; nor we to him. Victims of circumstance, we gazed sadly at each other over the chasm between.

Uncle Harry had two daughters, a little older than my sisters. His was a happy family. They had no reason to be otherwise, for they were free to be themselves. How do I remember him? In our drawing-room he used to sit at the piano, his head flung back, playing Gilbert and Sullivan, and other popular opera songs. The air would be fragrant with the scent of his best pipe tobacco, and he would sit there relaxed, singing in a melodious baritone, and fleetingly our troubles would melt away. When I stayed at his beautiful home in Sevenoaks, I would watch him leaning back in the tall winged armchair, gazing into the distance, discussing the affairs of the day, his great white Clumber spaniel at his feet. His family fell into place around him. Aunt Maggie, his wife, vivacious, busy, infinitely more sparkling than her sisters, used often to be overcome with mirth at his drolleries. There was a good deal of easy backchat, for he was *primus inter pares*, not the patriarchal figure on a pedestal.

He was tolerant and kind to me, a little amused at the presence of a small child I think, and he was my godfather, a relationship which dated from the private ceremony in the drawing-room in my infancy. If we were distant in age and understanding, yet on more than one occasion I had cause to be grateful to him for his intervention in my small affairs. There was the matter that began one day when I watched Lucy the parlourmaid go out looking smart in her dark green coat, and noticed her fair plaits wound around her head just visible under the neat little hat. Lucy had good taste coupled with a sheer respectability that was solid and stable. You could rely on her to do the right thing, to know the patients, and exactly what to say to them as she ushered them into the large consulting room each day. So it was a shock to everyone when she came back from that afternoon off totally changed. Her hair had been cut off, and was rather unattractively and artificially frizzed by a hairdresser with no artistry, and her pale earnest face had become quite ordinary. There were exclamations of dismay from the whole household. Only I was pleased. 'I like it, Lucy; you look more like a boy. I'm going to get mine cut off if I can. It's much better for us. I can't stand these long plaits.'

At the next meal I expressed pleasure at Lucy's appearance. My remarks got short shrift.

'The girl's entirely ruined', my father retorted. 'How incredibly foolish women are!'

I was dashed. It was clear the moment had not arrived for

me to raise my query. Later I consulted my uncle who was staying with us. His eyes twinkled and he nodded sagely: 'I quite agree', he said, 'it would never do to be behind the times! You must keep up to date.'

'Uncle Harry, my plaits give me headaches, and I want to look more like a boy. But only you can persuade Daddy to let me have my hair off. He believes hair is a woman's crowning glory', I told him.

'Well, I daresay it was for the Hebrews in Palestine in the first century AD, but that's no reason for it to be so in twentieth-century England', said my uncle.

Then winking in a solemn and conspiratorial manner, he added: 'This matter must be approached very carefully. Just leave it to me. I shall raise it at lunch-time. Just ask your mother to make an appointment at the hairdresser for you this afternoon.'

Uncle Harry did not say anything until lunch was nearly finished. Then he cleared his throat and gazed at the ceiling: 'Healthy fashion, this short hair for women, you know', he began ruminatively, 'all that stuff on their heads, very tiring. Far better to have it off.'

My father, who loved his brother-in-law, held different views in many matters, but each felt free to express his opinion. Now my father burst out in indignation: 'Really, Harry, how can you say that? It's a ridiculous, most unbecoming fashion. Women spoil themselves entirely. They look like men, quite repulsive, in fact.'

The argument waxed fast and furious, neither side giving way an inch.

'My dear old boy, even your mother had short hair, just look at the photographs', said my uncle vigorously.

'And it is a case of headaches, dear', said my mother, launching into the fray with the light artillery.

'Well, of course', said Uncle Harry, bringing up the heavy

cannon, 'how would *you* like all that weight on your head?
Unhygienic anyway. Most unreasonable.'

My father looked distressed, consulted his watch, and said
it was time he was in his consulting-rooms. But he came
back into the room, just as he was on the point of leaving,
and delivered the Parthian shot: 'I wash my hands of the
whole affair. But if you do this horrible thing, bring me
back your beautiful plaits.'

He departed. I flung my arms round Uncle Harry's neck.

'You're wonderful, Uncle Harry', I said, dancing up and
down.

'We shall have to be very circumspect', my uncle said
sagely, adding: 'Your father will get over this in time and
entirely forget about it.'

Later, as I sat wrapped in deep excitement at the hairdresser's, I watched the heavy tresses fall onto the floor
around me, and considered my father's extraordinary request.
I dismissed it as inexplicable, but being exhilarated with the
feeling of lightness and comfort, I felt charitable to all men,
and remembered to ask the barber for the plaited hair. He
was a wizened, silent man, who registered no emotion, only
an occasional rather bitter smile, which passed fleetingly and
a little alarmingly over his leathery features.

'Want to make a wig?' was all he said, as he handed me
the rather repulsive flat brown-paper parcel.

My father came up to the drawing-room at tea time. Uncle
Harry was smoking his pipe in a nonchalant manner. My
mother was fussing with the tea-cups on the shining brass
tray which stood on a little table in front of her. Nothing was
said at first. Then suddenly my father's eyes alighted on my
shorn head.

'Appalling!', he said, as he took a cup of tea, and not
another syllable passed his lips. In vain Uncle Harry dis-
coursed on the advantages, lauded the improvement. I was

now so chic, so comfortable, but my father said not a word. For a normally cheerful and happy man, he could only be judged to be sulking.

'Well, I've got those awful plaits for you', I said, stuffing the parcel into his hand. He carried it off, silently, wrapped in gloom. When he had departed, Uncle Harry chuckled a little.

'He's only registering his protest, really,' he said, adding 'it will be forgotten in a few days.'

And so it would have appeared. But years later, sent to look for something in my father's chest of drawers, I found among his treasures the flat paper parcel in a special place. On it, in the firm clear handwriting was the simple inscription 'M.A.'s plaits'. It was both funny and disconcerting. Searching for some understanding of this bizarre habit of hoarding odd useless articles which had only sentimental value, I am inclined to think the plaits of hair were for my father a symbol of the kind of girl he hoped I would be. His image of me was shaped by his unalterable loyalty to his Victorian home which had moulded him so firmly—a home where a woman was held in deep respect; he believed that her capabilities and talents should approximate to the dignity and beauty of the picture of the perfect wife in the Book of Proverbs, who was dutiful and distinguished, a talented woman who could manage the estates, purchase land, organise her household, dress them in scarlet cloaks in winter. She was assuredly a person of infinite variety and capabilities.

Image-making is a dangerous pastime. I think my father must have had a certain obstinacy in his refusal to relinquish preconceived ideas, and to adjust his views to fit in with other people's points of view. I was clearly in danger of being an anticlimax, inferior to all he hoped; a hoyden, a tomboy, a dreamer of dreams, impractical, impulsive, and now short-haired. The woman in Proverbs did me no service at all at that time, save to arouse a slight incredulity that one person could contain in herself such perfection. For sometimes we heard about her in the morning meeting on Sundays. She was a figure to be exalted as the type at which Brethren wives might aim. And even more trying was the often-quoted Pauline attitude to women. His strictures stated that their hair must not be braided in an unseemly fashion; they must be meek and docile to their husbands; their heads must be covered during a service—in case their hair became too distracting to the other sex I subsequently decided with a friend—and on no account must they be allowed to speak at a meeting for worship. Such a submissive paragon seemed outside of reality. Altogether it was really very tiresome, and I felt I just wanted to be myself.

14

THE CONFLICT

As I grew older, I was shut off from the world of both my sisters who, at this time, were carving out their careers. They were both tireless and conscientious in any work they undertook. Because their outlook was so different from that of my father it sometimes seemed, in a sense, as if they were outside a door, while I was inside, dependent on my father's strength and guidance. What sadness any sense of separation may have brought them, I can only guess. Both loved him. He was an attractive character is so many ways. But he could not comprehend their point of view, although always he wanted their happiness. But did he desire it on their terms or his? I cannot tell.

It was Easter that emphasised the differences between us. It seemed to mean so much to them. At first I really could not understand this because I had never celebrated this greatest of all festivals. Indeed, celebration was not a word whose meaning conveyed much to me.

My mother, sadly, as I think now, always bought us little gifts, putting them in small brightly-coloured cardboard eggs, which she placed beside our plates at breakfast on Easter Day. It was the only obvious concession in our home, for Plymouth Brethren celebrate no special days. I suppose such events are connected with Rome in their minds.

One year, my mother took me to stay with a cousin of my father's, a widower, who was a doctor in Surrey. Cousin John was part of the life of his village, knowing every man, woman and child. He was driven everywhere by Reed, his elderly chauffeur, little and old and rosy, like a pippin. Agnes the maid, and Cook looked after our cousin in the house. Each morning Agnes lovingly wrapped him in his muffler, and tried to persuade him to wear an extra cardigan if it was cold.

He was a pillar of the parish church. Quiet, kind and matter of fact, he regarded his faith as the stable secure foundation of life; but he would never have discussed the soul. So it was easy to be with him, even if his conversation was shy and a little unenterprising. 'Capital, capital', he used to say to any news my mother brought him. Or more seriously, 'Dear me, dear me'. So I summed him up as unemotional. Yet it was in his church that I first learned something of what my sisters had discovered, and there I first experienced what I can only call a joyful response of the spirit. It was certainly unexpected.

On Easter Sunday we woke up to a bright and brilliant day. Crossing the village green in the clear sunshine, and hearing the jangle of bells echoing joyfully across the fields in the clear air, I was conscious of a new sense of expectation. When we went inside the country church massed with spring flowers, and full of people who seemed ordinary and unsaintly, who lived in the open world outside my enclosed one, I suddenly and almost inexplicably knew happiness. I could worship here. I knelt, and listened entranced to the rolling triumphal notes of the organ. I had come to a place of beauty. I had never before heard the hymn 'Jesus Christ is risen today'. But when I heard it, such a climax of joy came to me that it was hardly to be imagined. Perhaps this seems strange now in an age where spiritual or religious feelings are discredited in a materialistic world. They are regarded as spurious; whipped up by the temporal excitement of a passing stimulus. And so we are denied the validity of the heart's response. It is a total inconsistency to decry true emotion. That Easter Day had for me a piercing reality. I was alive in a new dimension. I had a fleeting sense of the eternal.

The next year one of my sisters was unable to stifle her bitterness of feeling at my father's lack of interest in the great festival. In my family, matters that burned in the mind were apt to burst out. She argued with him on the basis of the great tradition of keeping this day, handed down for so many centuries from generation to generation, a time which had become so precious to all Christian people. Why then, she persisted desperately, did the Brethren feel it impossible to celebrate this greatest of all events? What arrogance made them assume they were right in denying the wisdom of all other Christians? Neither my father nor she could comprehend the attitude of each other. Both found the other side peculiarly blind. He reasoned quietly, not yielding an inch. She argued passionately, becoming more and more distracted at his refusal to move towards her opinion. It seemed barren and sad that Easter had brought a sword between them.

When she went by herself to the parish church with white set face, I remember noticing she looked very much alone. Everyone else seemed to be going in families. But we only, a family eaten up by the faith as it seemed to me, were split into rival factions. My father, my mother and I set off in the opposite direction to the Gospel Hall, with no enthusiasm on my part, and sadness on my parents' faces. It would not have mattered had it all been taken lightly; had each happily accepted the other's viewpoint. Was it love, then, between the members of the family that created the wish in them to draw the others into their circle of belief? They wanted, I am sure, to be at one. Yet neither side seemed able to perceive the significance of the others' belief which they found distasteful. The day that should have brought us together in unity and

joy set us apart in bitterness, and through it all my mother
walked in sorrow.

As I grew into adolescence, life sometimes seemed like a
great canvas painted in contrasting colours where sombre
darkness alternated with brilliant light, and the two were the
more intense for their coupling. Looking back, I believe we
were helplessly and irretrievably caught in a clash of character that none desired. There were often moments when storm
threatened, but when it broke in force it was unexpected, and
was only witnessed by the three people who were concerned.

I had begun to realise that my father's understanding of his
patients' needs, and his intense caring concern for them, was
not always matched by understanding of the hopes and fears
of others, of their joys and sorrows. Watching over his family
in love, and perhaps perplexity, he could not always discern
the emotions and needs of his children. Equally, they could
not comprehend his inflexible stand in matters of faith and
conduct. His standards were so high, his rules so demanding,
that they seemed at times impossible to accept. My sisters
belonged to a new generation emerging in bitterness or
doubt after the first world war, many of whom were dis-
illusioned, and many had thrown overboard old traditions
and customs and were moving uneasily into a new era. My
father was concerned to preserve ageless truth embodied in
biblical precepts which, as he interpreted them, were
applicable to all generations and all needs. He stood firm as
a rock, while the flood-tide of new thought, higher criticism,
radical rethinking of current beliefs, washed over him,
making no impression.

Our ways of thinking were all different, and because of
this, the strains sometimes became acute, for it was increasingly apparent that there was no neutral meeting ground of
understanding.

We were together in the lofty drawing-room one afternoon.

The beauty of the white marble Adam fireplace, the noble lion-skins on the soft blue carpet, and the great windows through which the late sun was flooding in, made a formal setting for my father's ordered life. By contrast, the pent-up emotions that poured out in wild disorder that day threatened to engulf us all. The dire clash of personalities, the opposing sorrows of people drawn to each other irrevocably in bonds of loyalty, yet irretrievably opposed in outlook, flowed out in a torrent of despair.

I was curled up in an armchair, reading, outside the circle, and one of my sisters and my father faced each other. My mother was an unwilling onlooker, and yet was unhappily drawn into the conflict. I do not even remember what began it, but my father was adamant in rejecting some wish of my sister. It may have been something that went against his conscience, I do not know. It was, in any case, the spark that started the fire. Her grief at his attitude, her hatred of his puritanism, her inability to make him understand her thoughts, and to make him realise that because he had married again, she felt much alone, must have been infinitely saddening to one who really needed him. That he was totally unaware of her deepest feelings, indeed was deeply concerned for her, made little difference. In that moment they faced each other as strangers.

My sister took a step forward, grief-stricken, angry, tortured: 'You give me nothing. You have no interest in what I do. You have left me alone. Your love is never given to me. Your religion is narrow, so impossible . . .'

She turned away, weeping bitterly. My father gazed at her aghast, his face tragic, its pallor accentuated.

'All I have is yours', he said, and the biblical words were like a cry of anguish. 'I have denied you nothing.'

'Only your love. You have none for me.' She moved quickly from him, and went to the door.

The three people left in the room stood frozen, motionless. It was my mother who stepped forward, arms held out, tears in her eyes. But my sister had gone.

My father gazed before him, unseeing. There was anguish in that look. He buried his face in his hands. Then silently, quietly, he went away. He had gone, I knew, to be alone, to commit the matter to the Lord who had all his heart, so that the glory of his vision had blinded him, in part, to the depths of loneliness of one who was desperate.

I was forgotten. I crept away to my room, and fiercely turned the stiff and jerky handle of the gramophone. Faster and faster I wound, and the slightly rasping trivial notes of 'The Bluebells of Scotland' echoed despairingly around me. They could not drown the sound of crying.

Later that evening, I lay on the haircord carpet, buried my head in my arms, and the burning fierce tears trickled down into the rough fibres and were received, accepted.

There was no one to comfort, no one to help. We were held captive in a fortress, built stone on faithful stone for conscience's sake by my father, who guarded it heroically, allowing no alièn deed or thought to undermine its foundations. He was a man, I saw now, who would die rather than allow anything to separate him from his God. It seemed as if, in the process, we were dying too.

My mother, withdrawn in her private grief, torn between love and loyalty to her husband and her awareness of the needs of others, now lay in a darkened room, not to be disturbed. I knew enough to realise her own private distress of mind, and I was distracted by the sadness of the day which had begun so brightly in my sun-filled room.

At last, as the light in the sky outside the windows mercifully dimmed into a soft grey dusk, the room was shrouded in a sort of oblivion. Slowly I drew a large diary towards me, in which I often poured out the stories and thoughts of a fertile imagination. But now I was minded to write the truth, to tell the impersonal unresponding page the sadness that was welling out, which could not be contained.

Lying on the floor I slowly began to write, while the pen scratched a little incongruously in the quiet desolate moment, and small soft splashes of tears impossible to restrain made the words coalesce and washed them almost away, and a sort of tired respite enfolded the mind. I lay, head on arm, silent. Only the clock ticked relentlessly, purposefully. Life would go on to new places, new situations. The gas fire hissed very softly, a muted reminder of warmth and comfort, and merciful darkness pressed against the pane.

It seemed hours later that the door softly opened. I neither spoke nor moved. My father stepped quietly into the tiny warm glow of the fire and sat down in a low chair beside me. I neither turned to him, nor showed any sign of recognition. At last he said very quietly, his voice infinitely sad: 'Remember, darling, we are not alone.' Later he rose and silently left the room. Still I did not move.

Outside the wind rose a little, and softly stirred around the old house which seemed to shelter those within it, to embrace them, and comfort a little.

15

SIXTEEN

It was a memorable year in odd contrasting ways. I remember the suffocating excitement of being allowed for the first time in my life to take part, with a small team of dancers, in a display of Swedish dancing at some garden fête in an old mansion near Bath. It was in aid of charity, I remember. What battle my mother had to fight to get my father's consent for me to do this I do not know. She had remained with him behind closed doors in the consulting-room for a long time. Perhaps she had guessed how despairing I felt at the restrictions placed on certain pleasures which were regarded as 'worldly' in Brethren circles.

The rhythm of traditional dance music filled me with wild excitement and joy, and I had begged, implored her to intervene on my behalf. I am sure no one else who watched the dancers in their colourful costumes that day could have guessed that a torrent of joy was pouring through the heart and mind of one of the team. It was liberation and acute happiness.

Emotion is apt to run unchecked in adolescent minds. One day you are a child still. The next you are changed, aware of new emotions, new desires. Life is a pendulum of hopes and fears, and one swings to and fro, neither here nor there. It is all Part of the process of leaving childhood behind.

What then is growing up? It is a heightened awareness, a quickening of the pulse, a sense of oneness with the universe.

197

It is to welcome all experience as part of a pattern of infinite variety and colour. It is to learn slowly and sometimes with pain to love and to accept.

Memory calls me back to a swiftly changing kaleidoscope of scenes of that year. There were carefree classroom days lying during the hot summer afternoons on the great lawns of the stone mansion on Lansdown, listening to the intensity of feeling of *Wuthering Heights*; hearing the magic of words in the hands of a craftsman; feeling the enchantment of Walter de la Mare's poetry; and all the while the heat burned down on to our backs, between the shoulder blades, and our stockinged legs were hot and restless. We vied with each other in playing with words, tossing them up and down like the bright balls of a juggler, experimenting, and creating. There were tedious days, too, wrestling at one's desk with Ovid and Virgil while the tantalising sun shone through the leaves of the great oak tree outside. There were happy days in the fields on the top of the hills surrounding Bath, running until the breath came bursting out of one's lungs, and the wind raced and chased the tall bending poplars and whipped in the face, and it was good to be young. Then came the cool stillness of the quiet ordered home where everything moved to the ticking of the clock, patients came and went, and my parents' voices were low and calm. Day followed day and outwardly there was peace.

It was shattered in a strange and unlikely way. I became one of the twice baptised. There cannot be many of us. Baptism is a mystery. To the Christian it should be a sacrament, a sign of a death that brings life, a resurrection experience. Various aspects of its sublime meaning are stressed by those with differing views. The attitude of the established church to those born within its fellowship follows the scriptural principle that whole families of believers may be baptised as members of Christ's family. Infants are brought in

anticipation that God will ratify His covenant promise to
His own, and that ultimately they may themselves make the
promises given on their behalf in infancy. But the Brethren,
like the Baptists and certain other sects, utterly refute the
validity of this belief, maintaining that baptism by immersion,
also Biblical, is necessary as an adolescent or adult and must
be an outward testimony to an inner change, a deliberate
affirmation of personal faith in Christ, the sign of a conversion
experience. The astonishing and saddening situation is that
men should maintain that only their own interpretation of
the truth is accurate or right. They usurp the position of God
in condemning the sincere and true conscience of others. They
persist in holding a position of total incompatibility with those
of differing views. But surely every man's true belief is held
as before God in these matters?

Baptism by immersion entered upon in deep conviction
and in faith can be for some a triumphant terrifying event,
a moment of awe and reverence signifying a deliberate death
of the self in repentance, and a re-birth into Christ through
His forgiveness. But by reason of the emphasis on the
need for the certainty of conversion, I was quite unable to
believe I could ever honestly be baptised, for I was conscious
of a sense of sin fostered in me from earliest years. Perhaps
this could have been therapeutic in that the knowledge of the
forgiveness of God brings ultimately a healing tide of relief.
But I had been present at baptismal services, when young
people were immersed in the waters of the open baptistry
which lay under the little platform used by speakers at the
Gospel meetings on Sunday evenings. As I saw them go
down the steps into the water—bravely and serenely it
seemed to me—in front of the large crowd which always
gathered for such a service, I was filled with terror. This was
something I could not face. I knew myself for a coward.
Somehow it was even more important not to be dishonest as

before God, and enter that water unworthily. Certain young people in the meeting seemed so safe, so secure in their belief, and a number were baptised from the age of twelve years and onwards. I had so often evaded my father's gentle question, 'Do you not feel you would like to join those at the Lord's Table?'. His anxious care made me feel a traitor of a sort; yet I knew I could not live with myself if I went through this service as a mere matter of form. My theology was clear, shallow and formulated by the belief that his views must be right. It was, I felt, necessary that one day I should want to enter into this experience. How I should come to it, I did not know. My happiness in the few Anglican services I had attended was purely sensuous at that time. I was not interested in rival doctrines. Insofar as I regarded them at all, I was sure that my father, whose faith worked so powerfully, must be nearer to God than those whose Christianity was nominal and, it must be admitted, ineffective by his standards. So while others went forward gladly to baptism, I never did, and I was disturbed to feel I could not join in this.

There came a Sunday when I was unexpectedly and gently led upstairs to the small room over the meeting hall by one of the elder Brethren after the morning service was over. Searchingly, kindly, and indeed with real concern, he asked me if I did not now feel the time had come to follow our Lord in the waters of baptism and make public confession of my faith. Ice-cold I considered the question, and knew my answer was the same. I was faced with a terrible dilemma. I believed that with my love of what I thought was 'the world', and my fear that I would fail in any promises made, I was totally unworthy to be baptised, or to come to the Lord's Supper on Sundays, or to join those whose faith was so clear, so free of doubts, and so devout. Somewhere I was lacking; I was, even here, an outsider, and must now be left out of the company of the saved, because I could not make vows I might not keep. What could I say? It was hard to explain my deliberate default.

The one thing I might have said, if I had had any understanding at the time, never entered my head, for no one ever reminded me of the event, nor did it seem of any significance. I could have said: 'I have already been baptised as an infant in the name of Christ, and no one and nothing can invalidate God's covenant promise claimed there for me.' But instead I stood silent, anxious, and had no answer.

'Is anything troubling you?' The voice was kind yet persistent. At last I said: 'I can't be baptised, because if I was it would have to be real.' A strange clouded answer, and it seems but yesterday I made it, so indelibly has the memory of that day remained.

To my shock, this was taken as a sign of grace and humility. I was told that this in fact signified I was ready. Now I did not know what to do. If I was baptised unworthily—as I knew I should be—I believed it would be a terrible sin, almost a blasphemy.

The date growing nearer and nearer, and the thought of the immersion in the baptistry in the crowded hall, and of myself not there as of right, bred a terror that I can remember yet. How sad that this was so. I truly believed that I, a sinner, should *not* be admitted to the fellowship of those who loved the Lord, because I knew that at any minute I would fail Him. I was unable to say a word of explanation, to ask any advice, I could not speak for the turmoil in my mind.

Another crisis now intervened. One of my sisters had been my godmother at my first baptism in infancy. She was deeply shocked to hear from my mother of the coming event. My mother, inescapably honest, had felt she must be told. Now there was warfare again. The sword thrust of anger and misunderstanding came along us, and I was the centre, the cause of it, powerless to stop the escalating clash of character

that ensued between those who fought for opposing principles.
I could not escape censure for my limited understanding. I
had never deeply studied the subject, tending to accept my
father's doctrinal views on the big issues of Christian faith if
not on matters of behaviour.

The evening came. The hall was packed with a sea of faces.
They swam before my eyes. In their happy certainties those
there only emphasised for me the realisation of my total
inadequacy. It was, I think, a moment so alone, so sad in its
fears and misunderstandings that to recall it is to feel the es-
sence of a deep and unforgotten grief. When I stepped down
into the cold and turgid waters, normally hidden, and now
opened up like a grave, deep and dark, there was anguish
in my mind, for I perceived so clearly I was unfit to be
there. I could only in sorrow ask for forgiveness.

Through the loud burst of singing that followed this immersion I was presently aware clearly and unexpectedly of a
new enfolding peace calming my distracted mind—and
suddenly I knew my prayer was heard.

I was barely conscious of all that followed later, the joyous
welcome, the handclasps, the loving embraces. The only face
I ever saw was my father's, shining with a joy I found poignant past words, as he saw his lamb brought into the fold.

16

THE PHYSICIAN

It was the physician to whom I was ultimately and irrevocably drawn. For, as the years passed, I watched his skill and compassion, and ever and again I saw a reflection of the One he served.

As I look back to the manner of his life, I remember how he got up at six-thirty or earlier each morning and had his time of quiet study and prayer. This rule was unalterable and never broken. He shut himself into his small dressing-room where he kept his devotional books, his Bibles, lexicons, his Old Testament in Hebrew, his Greek Testaments, and the Septuagint, and here he studied with intense concentration. Here, too, he knelt, day after day, and committed all the patients in his care to the healing power of Christ. The results were, of course, astonishing and absolute. His patients got better in many circumstances when it might, in the normal course of events, have seemed impossible. In the years I was at home, a death among them was rare. At one time he had so many long-standing patients over ninety years of age, in astonishingly good health and alert both physically and mentally, that it excited considerable comment. His practice of laying all the details of the day before God stemmed from his belief that in the Father's eyes nothing was too insignificant to be dealt with. So every decision, and some were difficult and weighty indeed, when there were no penicillin cures or antibiotic medicines, was thus put in a setting of consecrated thought and intercession, and never lightly or carelessly undertaken. The patient was, as it were, put into God's hands, with my father making himself the humble instrument of healing. The 'partnership', if one may reverently call it so, was formidable.

Sometimes as a girl I quietly turned that little brass door handle early in the morning, and looked inside, and he would be sitting there, wrapped in a rug over his dressing-gown if it was winter, gloves on his hands—he felt the cold, but it never deterred him—with his Greek New Testament open on his knee, a Concordance and a Greek grammar beside him, and a sharp pencil in his hand for jotting down any discoveries or thoughts about the meaning in the text.

He would look up at me absent-mindedly as the door opened, grey eyes glowing with some inner satisfaction at the fruits of his study.

'Oh, it's you, darling', he would say, 'come and listen to this.' Then he would read a verse or two of one of the Gospels, first in Greek, then in English.

'Say after me', he would add, 'Alpha, Beta, Gamma, Delta', and stumblingly I tried to learn the Greek alphabet, and make out some of the letters in the New Testament.

'You see, the meaning is so clear, so direct in the Greek, that it comes to us with such freshness,' he would explain, poring over the text, oblivious of the fact that I did not find his Biblical studies as exciting as he did. He was simply concerned to pass on his own enthusiasm and interest.

This early morning session alone, and in quiet, meant that my father began his day in an atmosphere of serenity. It was part of his belief that the day should be faced calmly and with the steady assurance that in all its difficulties God was beside him, and would hear any request for help and direction in every weighty matter.

It was this ability to live in 'the peace of God', and to lay.

before Him his troubles and perplexities, that bred his relaxed attitude to his work. It was strange that his deepest anxieties showed themselves over his children. But in his medical life he was not only at peace, but able to face problems with buoyancy, and his eyes were often full of hope and happiness. For it was no part of his belief that the day should be unnecessarily solemn, and that a doctor should be too serious at the bedside when the situation did not demand it. This serenity bred a sort of quiet merriment when things went well.

'I'm afraid poor John is so entirely lugubrious', he said once of a well-meaning colleague, 'that he nearly frightens his patients into the grave! I think it is essential to give their spirits a "lift", and to bring reassurance.'

So it was with frightened and nervous patients that he often exerted his humour and charm, and gently teased them out of their fears. On one occasion, when I felt very ill as a child, and was fearful that I might be in mortal danger, he laughed with much amusement:

'You have had many troubles, dear', he said, waving an admonishing finger at me, 'most of which have never happened! I think it is just possible that you may recover.'

Needless to say, I felt better at once.

He always found humour in certain episodes in his work, and these he would relate to my mother with enormous enjoyment, becoming so overcome with the funny aspect of his story that he laughed until the tears rolled uncontrollably down his cheeks. For his piety was mingled with a simple gaiety of spirit, and one never knew which would take the upper hand.

He was very fond of telling how he was summoned to visit the wife of a certain wealthy baronet in the dead of night. He was told he must on no account go in daylight, for no one must see him arrive. It appeared that this lady was a

Christian Scientist, and had broken her leg. She neither believed in illness nor doctors. Both were to be ignored. But strangely the leg grew worse. No one must therefore know of the perfidy to her faith, and no one must know she had sent for him. So my father went late at night to bring his medical skill to the one who refused to believe in it. He became quite a friend of the family, and various pleasant luxuries arrived from time to time, with the compliments of a grateful husband.

If he had a dislike, it was for neurotic women, with whom he showed patience, but inwardly felt much exasperation. On one occasion he became quite heated, and naming no names in front of me, he declared at the lunch-table that Mrs X must be a great trial to her husband. I immediately asked why.

'Because she insists he doesn't love her', said my father with a snort. 'In truth, I have never seen anyone so devoted, making himself such a doormat, and now he is very distressed, and she is hysterical. The lady has invented an entirely fictitious situation in her highly coloured imagination. Poor man! What a burden! It would be her fault if his affection did waver.'

I took silent note of what to avoid in marriage when grown up!

He sometimes recounted how a certain highly nervous woman needed her teeth extracted. Now my father was an expert at giving anaesthetics, having invented a certain method which was publicised in the British Medical Journal, and made for the safety and comfort of the patient. He often, therefore, assisted with his own patients when they had teeth removed. This particular lady was convinced she would perish during the proceedings. Just before she was given the anaesthetic, she moaned: 'If I don't ever come round, Doctor, it is all your fault!'

Much irritated my father said briskly, in relating the story: 'I felt this was an exceedingly unhealthy attitude in which to take an anaesthetic. So I bent down and shouted piercingly in her ear "When you come round, I shall expect the most ample apology!".

'It did the trick. On regaining consciousness, her first words through the tears induced by the "laughing" gas, were "Sorry, Doctor" and she appeared abject and penitent.'

His views on women were extremely Victorian. He thought their underwear totally inadequate and conducive to chills; he disliked make-up and lipstick and condemned it roundly as highly artificial. Yet he much enjoyed the conversation of lively intelligent women. To all he was considerate and courteous. In those days when class distinction still lingered on, certainly in Bath, he treated all who worked under him with great kindness and thoughtfulness. The matron of a big hospital told my mother on one occasion that the Doctor was very popular because he made her nurses feel 'like ladies', which was a somewhat wry comment on their position in the society of that day.

His way with children often succeeded where others had failed. The married son of a friend and colleague came to him much distressed on one occasion because his little boy appeared backward and unresponsive. He had been taken to more than one leading specialist, and all had said he was hopelessly retarded mentally. It was heart-breaking for the young parents, and they could hardly believe it. In great distress, they sought my father's professional help and advice. The little boy would make no contact with anyone, and did not speak; he suffered from hysterical outbursts, and although four years old, no one could get through to him.

My father went to the house, sat down in the sitting-room talking easily and cheerfully to the parents, who subsequently described the scene. The little boy watched him from the other side of the room. Presently my father took out his gold watch on its chain, and continuing to talk, casually swung it to and fro. Very slowly, the little boy came nearer, and soon was standing beside him, gazing at the watch. In a few minutes, with no effort or coercion, my father lifted him onto his knee, and let him play with the watch. Soon the little boy was leaning relaxed against him, calm and easy for the first time for long weary weeks. My father watched him intently, smiling and gently putting the watch first to one ear and then the other, played with him for a time, and the little boy began to laugh. Then drawing out coloured chalks and papers, he drew the child an orange: the little boy copied him, and produced his own orange, looking eagerly at my father for approbation. My father drew other objects; the little four-year-old copied him. They sat together for a long time, and at last my father gently put him down, having made certain tests, all of which the child had enjoyed with curiosity, although he never spoke. He had screamed when examined by other specialists.

My father told the parents that he had, in a way, good news for them. Their little son was extremely intelligent, far from mentally retarded, but he was entirely deaf, no sound whatever penetrating to him, and he was lost in a world of frustration and anxiety. It was inconceivable that this had not been discovered before, but such was the situation. My father, in giving himself entirely to the little boy, had established an immediate 'rapport'. As he went to the door to go, a touching scene ensued. The little boy rushed upstairs, re-appeared with a tiny suitcase packed with his treasures, took my father's hand, and tried to leave the house with him, and get into the car, ready to go away with the one man who had penetrated his loneliness and distress. It was the beginning of a friendship that lasted throughout my father's life. The boy never forgot him, and proved at a special school for the deaf to be exceptionally intelligent, and a little hearing was restored to him.

It was this ability to pour out the whole dynamic of his personality into his treatment of a patient that somehow drew a response out of them, and contributed to the healing. Once as a child, I had the opportunity, quite unexpectedly, of watching him at work in an emergency. A prominent citizen, a kind and charming man, at one time mayor of the city, who was a patient of my father's, was taken suddenly desperately ill in the street with a very serious heart attack, and appeared to be dying. A crowd gathered; the ambulance arrived and the man was lifted into it. Suddenly I saw my father's car draw up by the ambulance. With one bound, he seemed to leap out and into the ambulance, where his patient was lying, and he knelt down on the floor by the stretcher, and then and there began immediately to work to resuscitate the heart. I remember to this day the speed with which he flew into the ambulance, looking neither to left nor right, the deep intense concentration of his face as he knelt down, looking at the quiet figure. One had the impression that he was pouring himself, his healing power, his spiritual strength, right down into the sick man, and that every second was a concentrated battle. Needless to say, he saved his patient's life, and many were the generous presents he received, and heartfelt thanks from the man who had almost literally been brought back from the dead.

He was never at a loss when faced by some need, or by a slightly awkward situation. This could be amusing. A patient once described how a certain incident occurred when the room could not be made sufficiently dark for him to examine her mother's eyes, even when the blinds were drawn. Nothing daunted, he sent for a large umbrella, knelt on the bed, huddled under it with his patient, and peered into her eyes with his torch.

When sorrow came to a family, or anyone lay dying, my father often brought calm and peace when there might well have been despair. Once he walked a long distance in the snow to be with a dying man. The incident was always remembered by his wife and I was told: 'He brought wonderful words of comfort; I shall *never* forget them.'

It was, above all, the Medical Mission, which he started, that became a symbol in my mind of his gift for healing. In a plain unattractive little mission hall, in a poor area of the city, he gave his services free every Wednesday to those who could never have afforded specialist medical treatment. One of the aftermaths of the first world war was poverty in many places. Many people never went to a doctor. Panel doctors were greatly overworked. Patients often needed greater time to be given them and special attention which they could not afford. For this reason he enlisted the help of a dentist friend, and persuaded two of the aunts, Annie and Jennet, to join them, one in her capacity as a nurse, one to give tea to any who came, and to befriend them. Many were the poor people to whom he brought health and healing. He found large numbers needing surgery and was able to arrange this in the hospital where he was a consultant. He brought hope to many and in return they gave him their love.

He insisted on one thing, namely that at a fixed time there should be an evangelistic service during the day for any who cared to attend. This became very popular in that downtown area, where, as a result of his work, he became a well-loved friend in hundreds of poor homes.

I remember one Christmas an Italian woman coming to our home, whose family sold home-made ice cream off a barrow—'probably highly polluted', my father used to remark, for there were not then the regulations of hygiene and purity enforced that there are to-day. A great black-eyed creature, she stood self-consciously on our front door step, dressed in an ill-fitting coat pinned across her chest. She knew poverty, for she had an enormous merry family of dark-eyed children. But she had walked miles with a bright red geranium in a pot, which she could ill afford, to give to my father whom she loved; for 'he saved my life', she said simply as she handed it to my mother. When my father some years later nearly died, it was she who stood on the door step weeping, holding out for him a small bunch of gaily coloured flowers she had bought. 'There's no one like him', she said and her tears flowed freely down.

Each Sunday, the hall was used for mission services. My father was regularly asked to preach because of his connection with the area through the medical work. Generally he limited himself to one or two visits a year, feeling his talents lay in healing, not preaching. Because he was a well-known figure, many came just to hear him, to greet him, to shake his hand, and to thank him for all he had done for them. On these occasions I used to go with him.

It was generally the summer when we set out together from my home. He usually had very little spare time to take me out, and so it was like a brief holiday. Released from his medical responsibilities, he prepared to enjoy every minute of the walk. As I picture those days, the late afternoon sun was always slanting through the great trees in the park, casting long shadows across the grass. My father would gaze at the sky, note the cloud formations, smell the air, look about him, interested and alert to observe everything of interest. Here he would tell me the names of the different sorts of trees; there he would stop to pat the head of a dog, talk to a passing child, notice a bird in flight; and then with his sermon in mind he would begin to talk about the joys of the Christian life. He spoke as if our Lord was right there, living, walking beside us. Then we would leave the park, descend a hill to a depressing area, and walk through the gloomy back streets down to the sluggish dark green canal, lined by factories. We would approach the huge gasworks giving off noxious overpowering smells, and I would wrinkle my nose up, and feel we were entering a different terrain. Broken glass, orange peel, and bits of paper lay in the roadways; the drab houses had dark and often dirty windows; the curtains were dingy and hung haphazardly; and men in cloth caps slouched about at street corners, while women, arms akimbo, leant against the door posts shouting to each other; small grubby children, often without shoes or socks, played around their feet. Still my father would pursue his theme, and as we approached the hall, he invariably said in his simple way: 'Pray, darling, that I may speak only those words that our Lord shall give me, so that it may be to His glory.'

And gradually, among the smells and the squalor there, the thought began to occur to me that perhaps Christ could be found better here than in the superficial life of Bath society which I saw so often in the fashionable area in which I lived.

The remarkable thing was that his conversation was not forced or unnatural. I suppose some may have accused him of being obsessed with religion, but in fact it was something very much more than that. Conscious of his Master always beside him, he was not concerned with what men thought of him; he had found that which was, for him, ultimate truth, and nothing else mattered. His life was not, to him, in any way limited or narrow; rather it had an extra, a spiritual dimension, which made it so much fuller and more significant, that for him any other way was unthinkable. He had no interest in concerning himself with organisational 'religion'; or in 'turning on' a spiritual side. He simply regarded himself as totally available to the One whom at all times he served; and if, in the healing and comfort he brought to so many,

Christ worked through him, then he was an unimportant instrument; but in being used he found his ultimate happiness.

At last, the long walk over, the lowering sun now bathing the shabby rooftops in brilliant light, we arrived at the little hall where we were welcomed and led inside. It was invariably full for my father's visit, many having come just to see 'Doctor'. When he mounted the small platform and gave out the hymn, in his quiet clear voice, there was an immediate hush, an expectancy, and he would gaze down in love at many who owed their very lives to him.

The hymn was invariably the same. I have never forgotten it, and all these years later, it stirs deep memories. For in the shining kindness of his face as he read out the words of the first verse, I seemed to see clear and strong a reflection of the love of Christ:

> 'At even, ere the sun was set,
> The sick, O Lord, around Thee lay;
> Oh, in what divers pains they met!
> Oh, with what joy they went away.'

'The door of the great house where I grew up is closed now.
I shall not enter there again.'

17

LAST PICTURES OF A FAMILY

ONE night rather over a year before the Second World War broke out, my father fell unconscious to the floor, having returned from a late night visit to a patient. From an illness lasting two years, he emerged an old man. Often I sat beside him when I came home from the north of England where I was working, and he would laugh at my stories of what it was like to be a raw teacher in a school, and at my rather turbulent life—or so it seemed after the smooth ordered days in a professional home in Bath, and at London University. He had fought his illness as steadily and as vigorously as he pursued his faith. Almost given up for dead, he amazed his medical advisers by returning to life with unbelievable determination and patience. Saddened by the sale of his practice, the handing over of his patients to another man, the loss of his maids who had all been part of his household, by the sale of the car which he had so enjoyed driving, he nevertheless hid his regrets, and calmly accepted life in a small rented house in a quiet undistinguished district.

By the time the Second World War had reached a climax at the fall of Dunkirk, he had at last regained a surprising measure of strength and he decided he must play his part again. Incredible as it seemed to his family, he consented to go back as visiting physician to the large local orthopaedic hospital while other doctors were away in the forces. He was delighted to have this work, and threw himself into it with a temporary surge of astonishing vigour. He now had many children in his care once more, and this was a great joy to him. It was an Indian summer. He had no car, he was poor financially, and he walked a long distance to and from the hospital each day, only occasionally consenting to take a bus. The matron described him in a letter written later:

'He was beloved by all, sisters, nurses and patients alike, even to the little ones, to whom he was so kind and gentle. We all appreciated working for him, and his wisdom and unfailing courtesy must have influenced many a young nurse starting out in her career.'

As he walked to and fro, enemy aircraft often passed overhead. He was not disturbed. He gazed at the sky unafraid for himself. It was God's world, and one day in the future 'sorrow and sighing would flee away', for those who loved the Lord would join him at his Second Coming. Unlike many of the Brethren, he did not often talk about this belief, yet it was a hope that was lively within him. As a boy he had had his own fears, for he once wrote to me:

'Like you, the second coming of the Lord Jesus Christ has had an element of dread in it, as I remembered my many sins and shortcomings.'

But now it was different. Man in his dire enmities he felt could only be at peace when the Lord returned.

But one night in 1942, as I recounted in another book, his home, his garnered treasures, his books, his medical instruments, were all destroyed in a moment of time during a savage air raid on Bath, and with my mother he struggled from the wreckage wounded in the head, knowing that now he had nowhere to call his own. From that ordeal he emerged frail, his spirit unquenched. But his working days were over. In one sense the war finished his life. In this he was not alone.

On the night of the raid the two remaining aunts sat quietly together in their rooftop flat. Aunt Edith lay bed-ridden and helpless, unable to move. Aunt Jenny, now very delicate, sat holding her hand. Annie, the vigorous and cheerful sister, had died some years before, as had Mary after a long twilight illness. Together the two aunts waited quietly there, and committed themselves to the Lord. In the middle of the night a high explosive bomb shook the whole house to its foundations, cracking the walls and the ceilings, and tearing down plaster. When morning came, they were still alive in a house that was so damaged that eventually it had to be evacuated. Like their brother they were homeless.

It was now that the elder daughter of Uncle Harry and Aunt 'Maggie'—both of whom had died peacefully before the war in their beautiful home within a short time of each other—sent for the aunts to come to her by ambulance. She had inherited all her father's staunch loyalty to the family. Working at London University and living with her sister, she was now the only one of the immediate family to have a suitable home for them. When Aunt Jennie was carried into the ambulance and left her brother on whom her deepest affection was set, and on whose broad shoulders she had so often leaned for comfort and strength, I think she quietly broke her heart.

My cousins cared for the aunts with great kindness. But they lived in an area where there was the constant fear of enemy attack. Eventually Aunt Jennie loosened her hold on life, and returned in mind to the days of the past. She thought she was a child at Blackheath, and again and again she called for the mother and father who in a way, I believe, she had never left. At last her tired spirit, unable to cope with the world in which she lived, flickered and went out, and she was at rest.

My Aunt Edith alone of the seven sisters was left. Many

called her an indomitable woman. Her pioneer journeys in China had been made with sheer determination and physical courage. She still faced her helplessness with the same stoical and almost inhuman calm. Only with my father did she ever permit the mask to be removed, so that he alone knew the unceasing pain she suffered. She only, I think, was his equal. The others had relied on him, depended on his counsel and judgement, and looked to him for leadership. Aunt Edith had an almost masculine control, and an iron will. Some inner resource held her steady and unflinching, and her hold on life was strong. After the war was over, she was brought back to Bath to live with a nurse who cared for her during the years left to her.

The war years had left their mark on my father and mother. The world as they knew it had vanished, and life could never be the same again. For over a year they lived in an attic in a friend's house. At last they found, after weary endless searching, a rather shabby maisonette to rent, and here they settled. Its walls were a little cracked, but it was near the Royal Crescent, and the outlook was pleasant. They were back on home territory for the last years of life.

My mother, shaken by the violence of events, gave up all outside work to be with my father; and I believe it was at this point that she lost heart. When I returned home at rather infrequent intervals, she was sad, sometimes depressed in spirit, and anxious about my father.

'I can't bear to see him so weak', she said as he often became ill; and I saw that life without him was something she was unable to face. Her strength, her independence had gone.

I sometimes think she may have secretly questioned whether she had done right in following my father's path. This uncertainty had a subtle corrosive effect on her mind. Over the years, with grief I had watched her retreat steadily into an inner world of regret and uncertainty, and the physician beside her had no power to heal a broken spirit.

Surrounded by books of spiritual consolation, I think she struggled to fortify her faith, to gain my father's serenity, and from time to time her vitality seemed totally quenched. In her own eyes she was a failure. With the tiredness of spirit came physical weakness. Caring for my father, and nursing him, she was slowly and surely drained of all strength.

One of my sisters was able to visit our parents regularly. The other was married to a scientist doing important research work, and only saw my father very occasionally. Differing outlooks could not, however, destroy the ultimate relationship between father and daughters. We all shared distress to see him growing steadily weaker.

As he lay in bed, he studied eagerly the latest antibiotic treatments, and other fascinating developments in medicine. Straining his failing eyesight over the *British Medical Journal*, he looked up at me one day with a shamefaced smile: 'I *must* keep up to date', he remarked.

I was now married and living in the north of England and had a very young family to care for. In the spare time my father found so strange, he began to write regularly to his little grandchildren in whom he took a delighted interest. To one of them he wrote:

> 'I send you a picture of the little bunnies going up to bed, and their mother holding the candle to light them up the stairs. Outside the window you see what a beautiful starry night it is, and you see the little bunny telling his mother. I daresay the eldest bunny boy is saying to his mother "Wouldn't it be nice to go out and look at the stars instead of going to bed?".'

And in the words I thought there was an echo of the little boy at Blackheath. He also wrote to me. His lively mind was

still eager for knowledge, and he described some of the
varied books he had read:

> 'medical books, some fiction, a little history, and also some
> Bible-reading with one of Archbishop Trench's books on
> "Miracles".'

The variety was typical.

On his good days he was driven up to sit beside his sister
Edith. The almost fierce and protective bond between them
never weakened, for they were irrevocably united to each
other as members of the same family. They shared the same
faith, they looked to a day of relief from their weakness, and
to future joy when they should see their Lord. My father was
stricken to see the extreme suffering of his sister, writing to
me when she lay very ill that 'she did so wish "to depart and
be with Christ which is far better".' Not long after this, he
wrote to tell me that she had, at long last, 'fallen asleep', and
he could do no other than be thankful.

And now, slowly but steadily, he turned his own thoughts
to what must come. He was the last, the only one of that
family of eight children, so vivid, so hopeful, so eager for life.
He had sat beside six of them when they were dying, and
his mind was set to tell me his own final thoughts that must
now be passed on:

> 'On reading St John 14 many times recently I think I can
> see some fresh light. Read it again, verse 2 "I go to prepare
> a place *for you*", and then verse 3 "And if I go and prepare
> a place for you, I will come again and receive *you unto
> Myself* that where I am there *ye may be also*". Is it not
> almost beyond imagination? It is like the "Peace of God"
> which "passeth all understanding". Read this daily. I
> often repeat it to myself before going to sleep.'

Away in the north of England I read this letter many times

until the paper became thin and tattered and the writing almost undiscernible.

At length when he himself was bedridden, and nearly blind, there was no one to nurse him, for my mother had no longer the strength. She herself was now a sick woman. He was taken to a large geriatric ward in a hospital on the outskirts of the city. It had been the workhouse. It seemed that for this man who had, perhaps, done more in the city for medicine in his time than any other, no comfort could be found.

A friend who had faithfully stood beside my parents in their last years went to see him.

'Oh, *why* did they send you *here*?', she asked.

Perhaps he was dreaming. Or could it be that he was thinking of the divine precedent when he answered:

'There was no room for *Him* in the inn.'

Many things were written of my father after his death. The *British Medical Journal*, after describing his medical achievements, wrote:

'His one aim in life was to serve his fellow man, and in doing so he encouraged others to follow his example.'

A close friend, a well-known specialist, wrote of him in the press:

'He was a man of noble and generous disposition, ever ready to help, and who gave of his time and skill unsparingly where need existed. His whole life was spent in the service of others. One never appealed to him in vain, whatever the subject. As a physician his opinion was much sought, for his work was marked by a meticulous attention to detail, and a thoroughness that could not but add to the weight of the opinion he expressed. I well remember a patient, both blind and deaf, for whom his opinion and

help was sought, saying to me the morning after the consultation, "Who is that man who has been all through my
being?".'

He was also described in the local paper by one of his
patients:

'He was a very good doctor, able, experienced, almost
uncannily successful. He would have said he was but the
medium through which his Master, the Great Physician,
worked.'

That perhaps touched the heart of the matter. In his work
he had achieved great things because he had learned to give
only his best, and then to leave all he did in the hands of
Christ.

Less than a year after my father's death, my mother also
died. Her life virtually had ended when he left her.

In the development of character I saw around me through
the years she was to me a central figure. She made the setting
against which my father exercised his talents, so that his
achievements shone the more brightly. Her own work for
education, her interest in the many young people who never
came to her in vain for help, were never stressed, and rarely
mentioned. At times I felt she hid many of her thoughts, and
I feared for her. She had identified herself completely with
my father, and they had shared many things.

She was my rock. Where I was ebullient, she was calm
and controlled. Where I was headstrong, impetuous, hasty,
she was wise and careful. When I was sad, she would comfort. I often thought she had given up much to marry. But
when I told her this, she laughed, and said: 'Oh, no! I am
one of the lucky ones.'

Shortly before she died, she gazed at me with sad and
clouded eyes: 'What do you think will happen to me in

heaven?', she said wistfully. 'He will have gone to his first wife, and I shall be forgotten.'

There was a world of desolation in her voice. I looked at her and saw a face grown thinner. I saw the magnificent intellect dimmed into the mind of a lonely child who had suffered grievous loss. In her clouded thoughts the years had rolled back, leaving the kernel of apprehension, sensitivity and fear which she had fought steadily to overcome.

I put my arm around her.

'No, you won't be left', I said. 'Don't you remember that Jesus said there would be no marriage or giving in marriage there? It will be a place of blessed happiness, and all misunderstandings will have gone. Don't you remember the words, "God shall wipe away all tears from their eyes"?' I held her as if she was a shaken child, and she smiled dimly and distantly and fell silent. She never spoke of this again.

Not long after, she died in hospital while I was in the train on my way to her. She had called for me again and again, they told me. We never said the last goodbye. Perhaps it had been said already.

It was summer when I left her, lying there beside my father on the hillside. We had sung the words she asked for, as they had for him:

> 'Goodness and mercy all my life
>   Shall surely follow me,
> And in God's house for evermore,
>   My dwelling-place shall be.'

18

TOWARDS AN ANSWER

THE album is closed now. The joys and sorrows which it has uncovered must fade again into the past where they belong.

Sometimes I hear in imagination those voices again, strengthening, comforting, consoling. Or I hear the words of the hymn they used to sing together, as one after another they took up the tune in harmony, and I am stirred with a feeling I cannot express, for I saw true joy on their faces:

> 'Were the whole realm of nature mine,
>   That were an offering far too small;
> Love so amazing, so divine,
>   Demands my soul, my life, my all.'

Yes. They were prepared to be laughed at, scorned, forgotten by the world. They had seen a vision which carried them through life. It coloured their thinking, garrisoned their hearts in anguish and loss, captivated them in time of happiness, and held them unflinching on their pilgrimage and, because of them I have glimpsed it too.

So there is no easy answer. I cannot produce neat formulas, doctrinal statements, to explain the sorrow I saw, or put it in a favourable light; I can only face it and fight for understanding.

Here I saw the bitterness of division between people who loved each other. Insofar as they could not understand each other, or accept each other's beliefs and convictions, they

224

were hurt, at times almost beyond repair. Yet there was not one of them who did not seek goodness in some form or other, even if unconsciously. In the clash of character I saw, goodness and evil seemed to meet and sometimes it was hard to disentangle the two.

As I recalled all that happened, I saw how barriers of the spirit divide and threaten to destroy us. Those who walk in separation will always know grief and tragedy, whether in a family or among friends. It is this which causes the world to point the finger of scorn: 'See how those Christians love one another!' And men turn away cynical, disinterested. How, then, can we reach out to each other?

Perhaps we have first to learn to accept men as they are, acknowledging that in the depth of their being good and evil do meet and war together. This is the duality of man's spirit; this is the price of his full humanity, his freedom. This indeed, is where we are at the very level of existence where God works out his redemption. Here is a faith that is not blind for this is the point of reality.

This is why I do not believe it is our primary task to be restlessly concerned to change people, or even, *at first* to bring them to our own belief, unless it is their desire. For this is to be dissatisfied with them as they are. It is this which destroys relationships, alienates parent from child, friend from friend. I am convinced that we have first to learn the longer, harder way of real love, for this, alone, is the dynamic power that can eventually restore, renew and heal. This was Our Lord's way; the disciples only came slowly to belief as they lived beside him.

And so we have come to the heart of the problem. As I returned to an old story of the past, I saw it was repeated in many places and in many ways today, and all the questions it asked me were bound up in one—'What is love?' It was only when I began to see those days through the eyes of others that I glimpsed the beginning of an answer, and, hesitatingly, I must now say: Love is total acceptance. It is a holding out of the hands in welcome.

It is having no preconceived idea of what you wish a person to be, or how you wish to alter him.

It is first to be waiting for him just as and where he is.

It is to stand beside the sick, the lonely, the desperate, and the delinquent, and to see life with *their* eyes; and there, in humility, to be available to Christ, Who alone can transform us, so that through us his power can reach out to those in need.

If they are changed through love, then that is what happened to Peter and Paul, and countless others.

For it is *reconciliation*.

But first we must take our stand at a Cross and listen to the cry which has echoed down the centuries:

'Father, forgive them; for they know not what they do.'

This only is the place where good triumphed over evil so that our healing might be accomplished. For here our brokenness, our blindness, our cruelties, and our misunderstandings are received, accepted, and forgiven, so that in the fullness of time there may be Resurrection.

BIBLIOGRAPHY

Mr Guy's Hospital, H. C. Cameron, Longmans.
Illustrated Social History, G. M. Trevelyan, Pelican.
Essays and Miscellanies, John Hollinshead, published 1866 in 'To-Day'.
Charles Kingsley, Letters and Memories of his Life, edited by his wife (1879), C. Kegan Paul.
Glaucus, or the Wonders of the Shore, Charles Kingsley.
Alive and Well, Norman Longmate, Chivers–Penguin Library Edition.
Illustrated History of the South-Eastern Railway and its Branches, George Measom (1858), reprint, E. & W.
Victorian and Edwardian London from old Photographs, John Betjeman, Batsford.
The Victorian Church, Owen Chadwick, A. & C. Black.
A History of the Church in England, J. H. Moorman, A. & C. Black.
A History of the Brethren Movement, Roy Coad, Paternoster Press.
A History of the Plymouth Brethren, W. Blair Neatby (1901), Hodder & Stoughton.
The Water Babies, Charles Kingsley, Macmillan.
The Gobi Desert, Mildred Cable with Francesca French, Hodder & Stoughton.
Protestant Island, Sir Arthur Bryant, Collins.
Victorian Cities, Asa Briggs, Odhams.
The Life and Explorations of F. S. Arnot, Ernest Baker, Seeley Service.
Elizabeth Garrett Anderson, Jo Manton, Methuen.
Edwardian England 1901–1914, edited by Simon Nowell-Smith, Oxford University Press.
Churches and the Working Classes in Victorian England, K. S. Inglis, Routledge & Kegan Paul.
Victorian Panorama, Peter Quennell, B. T. Batsford.
Brooke Fosse Westcott, Life and Letters, edited by Arthur Westcott (1903), Macmillan.
Evil and the God of Love, John Hick, Collins.
The Outsider, Colin Wilson, Pan Books.
The Evangelicals, John King, Hodder & Stoughton.
The Parting of Friends, David Newsome, John Murray.